Roz Shafran has worked at Oxford on the treatment of eating disorders using CBT. She currently works as the Charlie Waller Chair in CBT at the University of Reading. She is the author of *Cognitive Behavioural Processes across Psychological Disorders: A Transdiagnostic Approach to Research and Treatment* (Oxford University Press).

Dr Sarah Egan is Director of the Clinical Psychology program at Curtin University in Perth, Australia and is also the Australian representative of the World Congress of Behavioural and Cognitive Therapies committee. She continues to work as a clinical psychologist in private practice.

Professor Tracey Wade teaches at the School of Psychology at Flinders University in Adelaide, Australia. She is also Course Director of the university's Clinical Postgraduate training programs and has worked as a clinician treating eating disorders for the past 20 years.

The aim of the **Overcoming** series is to enable people with a range of
common problems and disorders to take control of their own recovery program.
Each title, with its specially tailored program, is devised by a practising
clinician using the latest techniques of cognitive behavioral therapy –
techniques which have been shown to be highly effective in changing the
way patients think about themselves and their problems.
The series was initiated in 1993 by Peter Cooper, Professor of Psychology
at Reading University and Research Fellow at the University of Cambridge
in the UK, whose original volume on overcoming bulimia nervosa and
binge-eating continues to help many people in the USA, UK, Europe and Australasia.
Many books in the **Overcoming** series are recommended by the UK Department of Health
under the Books on Prescription scheme.

Other titles in the series include:

All titles in the series are available by mail order.
www.overcoming.co.uk

OVERCOMING PERFECTIONISM

A self-help guide using
Cognitive Behavioral Techniques

ROZ SHAFRAN, SARAH EGAN AND TRACEY WADE

ROBINSON
London

Constable & Robinson Ltd
3 The Lanchesters
162 Fulham Palace Road
London W6 9ER
www.constablerobinson.com

First published in the UK by Robinson,
an imprint of Constable & Robinson Ltd, 2010

A copy of the British Library Cataloguing in
Publication data is available from the British Library

Important Note
This book is not intended as a substitute for medical advice or treatment.
Any person with a condition requiring medical attention should consult a
qualified medical practitioner or suitable therapist.

ISBN: 978-1-84529-742-8

Typeset by TW Typesetting, Plymouth, Devon
Printed and bound in the EU

1 3 5 7 9 10 8 6 4 2

Table of contents

Acknowledgments

This book brings together many years of clinical practice and training in the treatment of psychological problems across the world. We are indebted to the people whose work has inspired us and has contributed directly or indirectly to the strategies presented in this book. In particular we acknowledge the contribution of A. Beck, J. Beck, D. Burns, Z. Cooper, M. Fennell, C.G. Fairburn, S. Rachman, G.T. Wilson and Christine Padesky. We are also very grateful to the numerous clients who have shared their stories with us, and trusted us to help them get better. Overcoming their difficulties is what inspires us to continually develop new ways to help those who struggle in their daily lives. Finally, we would like to thank our families and friends, who know we're not perfect but accept us anyway.

Foreword

Why a cognitive behavioral approach?

The approach this book takes in attempting to help you overcome your problems with perfectionism is a 'cognitive-behavioral' one. A brief account of the history of this form of intervention might be useful and encouraging. In the 1950s and 1960s a set of therapeutic techniques was developed, collectively termed 'behavior therapy'. These techniques shared two basic features. First, they aimed to remove symptoms (such as anxiety) by dealing with those symptoms themselves, rather than their deep-seated underlying historical causes (traditionally the focus of psychoanalysis, the approach developed by Sigmund Freud and his associates). Second, they were scientifically based, in the sense that they used techniques derived from what laboratory psychologists were finding out about the mechanisms of learning, and they put these techniques to scientific test. The area where behavior therapy initially proved to be of most value was in the treatment of anxiety disorders, especially specific phobias (such as extreme fear of animals or heights) and agoraphobia, both notoriously difficult to treat using conventional psychotherapies.

After an initial flush of enthusiasm, discontent with behavior therapy grew. There were a number of reasons for this, an important one of which was the fact that behavior therapy did not deal with the internal thoughts which were so obviously central to the distress that many patients were experiencing. In particular, behavior therapy proved inadequate when it came to the treatment of depression. In the late 1960s and early 1970s a treatment for depression was developed called 'cognitive therapy'. The pioneer in this enterprise was an American psychiatrist, Professor Aaron T. Beck. He developed a theory of depression which emphasized the importance of people's depressed styles of thinking, and, on the basis of this theory, he specified a new form of therapy. It would not be an exaggeration to say that Beck's work has changed the nature of psychotherapy, not just for depression but for a range of psychological problems.

The techniques introduced by Beck have been merged with the techniques developed earlier by the behavior therapists to produce a therapeutic approach which has come to be known as 'cognitive behavioral therapy' (or CBT). This therapy has been subjected to the strictest scientific testing and has been found to be highly successful for a significant proportion of cases of depression. It has now become clear that specific patterns of disturbed thinking are associated with a wide range of psychological problems, not just depression, and that the treatments which deal with these are highly effective. So, effective cognitive behavioral treatments have been developed for a range of anxiety disorders, such as panic disorder, generalized anxiety disorder, specific phobias, social phobia, obsessive compulsive disorders, and hypochondriasis (health anxiety), as well as for other conditions such as drug addictions, and eating disorders like bulimia nervosa. Indeed, cognitive behavioral techniques have been found to have an application beyond the narrow categories of psychological disorders. They have been applied effectively, for example, to helping people with weight problems, couples with marital difficulties, as well as those who wish to give up smoking or deal with drinking problems. They have also been successfully applied to dealing with low self-esteem.

Problematic perfectionism, like low self-esteem, puts individuals at risk of developing a range of psychological disorders and, similarly, occurs as a symptom of several conditions. Perfectionisms (the beliefs that perfection can, and should be, attained) can constitute a problem in their own right, but also, when present as a feature of other psychological disorders (for example, eating disorders), they can complicate the treatment of that disorder. This book describes why people become perfectionists and discusses the problems that this causes for them. It also provides clear and accessible guidelines for overcoming perfectionism (without lowering individuals' standards).

The starting-point for CBT is the realization that the way we think, feel and behave are all intimately linked, and changing the way we think about ourselves, our experiences, and the world around us changes the way we feel and what we are able to do. So, for example, by helping a depressed person identify and challenge their automatic depressive thoughts, a route out of the cycle of depressive thoughts and feelings can be found. Similarly, habitual behavioral responses are driven by a complex set of thoughts and feelings, and CBT, as you will discover from this book, by providing a means for the behavior, thoughts and feelings to be brought under control, enables these responses to be undermined and a different kind of life to be possible.

Although effective CBT treatments have been developed for a wide range of disorders and problems, these treatments are not currently widely available; and, when people try on their own to help themselves, they often, inadvertently, do things which make matters worse. In recent years, the community of cognitive behavioral therapists has responded to this situation. What they have done is to take the principles and techniques of specific cognitive behavioral therapies for particular problems, and present them in manuals which people can read and apply themselves. These manuals specify a systematic program of treatment which the person works through to overcome their difficulties. In this way, cognitive behavioral therapeutic techniques of proven value are being made available on the widest possible basis.

The use of self-help manuals is never going to replace the need for therapists. Many people with emotional and behavioral problems will need the help of a qualified therapist. It is also the case that, despite the widespread success of cognitive behavioral therapy, some people will not respond to it and will need one of the other treatments available. Nevertheless, although research on the use of these self-help manuals is at an early stage, the work done to date indicates that for a great many people such a manual is sufficient for them to overcome their problems without professional help. Sadly, many people suffer on their own for years. Sometimes they feel reluctant to seek help without first making a serious effort to manage on their own. Sometimes they feel too awkward or even ashamed to ask for help. Sometimes appropriate help is not forthcoming despite their efforts to find it. For many of these people the cognitive behavioral self-help manual will provide a lifeline to a better future.

Peter J. Cooper
The University of Reading, 2010

Introduction

Is this book for you?

When you hear someone say 'She is such a perfectionist' or 'He just has to do things perfectly', it can be said with either a degree of envy or a degree of exasperation. On the one hand, we admire people who strive for high standards and a high-quality product. On the other hand, we are frustrated by people who persist in perfecting tasks and attending to detail in a way that makes a task take longer without adding substantially to the final outcome. Typically people who fall into this latter group are also causing distress to themselves, as they agonize over the detail of what they are doing and worry about how it might be received. Sometimes they lose confidence in their ability to deliver a worthwhile outcome, whether in work, social situations, leisure pursuits, sport, study or appearance. This type of perfectionism can result in self-criticism, lowered self-esteem and impaired performance. If perfectionism is having any of these consequences in your life, then this book is for you.

This book may be useful not only for anyone who identifies perfectionism as being a problem for them, but also for those with family or friends who have unhelpful perfectionism. It might be that perfectionism is causing problems in itself, or that it is associated with other problems like anxiety, depression or eating difficulties. We emphasize throughout this book that perfectionism is not simply having high standards but relates to one's self-esteem being too dependent on striving and achievement, and that this brings with it a range of difficulties. The good news is that this sort of unhelpful perfectionism can be changed without you necessarily achieving less.

The aim of this book

The aim of this book is first to help you to understand perfectionism, and then to suggest ways to overcome it. It is divided into two parts. Part One is about understanding perfectionism. In this section you will learn about what perfectionism is, what problems it can cause and keep going, and why it develops and persists. Part Two is about learning how to change your perfectionism. This section will help you to understand how it is that *your* perfectionism persists, to consider the costs and benefits, and to learn how to monitor your perfectionism. The strategies we describe for learning to overcome perfectionism include challenging unhelpful behaviors and thoughts related to perfectionism, tackling self-criticism, and broadening and strengthening your self-worth so that it is not based just on achievement. This is *not* about lowering your standards; it *is* about helping you stand back to consider what you want from your life, and whether your existing strategy (striving for achievement) is helping you or hindering you from reaching your goals.

Throughout the book we use examples based on cases we have seen and treated for perfectionism over the years. Although of course the names and some other details have been changed for reasons of confidentiality, these are all based on real individuals; we hope that you will see your own difficulties reflected in their circumstances, and also that their stories of recovery will help inspire you to begin to make changes to your own life.

How to use this book

We strongly recommend that you not only read this book, but also do some of the tasks we suggest in Part Two, as it takes some practice in doing things differently to change habits and ultimately overcome a problem. It is useful to read Part One first before going on to practice the tasks in Part Two, so that you have a better understanding of how perfectionism can be a problem and why. This book is a self-help approach to overcoming perfectionism; however, if you are having particularly strong difficulties, or experience trouble implementing some of the changes suggested in Part Two, it may be worth finding a therapist who can give you personal help in overcoming your perfectionism. Alternatively, if you are trying the techniques but they are not helping you as much as you would hope, then again we suggest you look for a therapist to help guide you through the book or to give you a different form of therapy.

One word of warning! People with perfectionism can try to approach all tasks in their life in a 'perfect' manner. For some readers, that will include the exercises in this book. We have worked with perfectionists who spend hours on their 'homework' between therapy sessions, trying to get it 'right'. We have also worked with perfectionists who keep putting off doing the homework because they feel they can't do it perfectly, and therefore they avoid committing pen to paper. In the same way, as you work through this book you might feel that you have not done your 'homework' – the various exercises and worksheets – 'right', 'properly' or 'well enough'. So we would like to emphasize at the outset: *there is no particular right or wrong way of doing the tasks* (Section 7.5 on 'all or nothing thinking' is relevant here immediately!). We advise you to aim for a middle way, because that is what we think will yield you most benefit from this book. We suggest, as a guideline, that you work through the book according to a flexible plan, perhaps aiming to cover a chapter a week, setting aside time to read each chapter and absorb its content, complete the exercises, and set yourself some realistic goals that arise from the chapter for the week ahead. You are most likely to remember to do this if you plan to set aside the same piece of time each week for this, for example a Wednesday evening. Just as importantly, set yourself an approximate limit for how long you will spend reading the chapter and doing the exercises. As you work through the book, keep in mind some important principles:

- There are no 'right' answers or 'wrong' ways of doing things. The exercises are designed to help you to apply the ideas in this book to your individual situation, and so the form of the exercise will look different for each person. They are intended to get you thinking about how to make changes in *your* life.
- The most critical point for producing change in your life is not how well you complete the pen and paper exercises but to what degree you practice the ideas each day and experiment with change.

We welcome you to the beginning of change.

PART ONE

Understanding Perfectionism

1

What is perfectionism?

'Perfectionism' is a term that is used commonly in everyday life. People often refer to a perfectionist as someone who strives to achieve their best performance and goals in everything they do. Perfectionism can be present in every aspect of life. Someone may be a perfectionist in just one part of their life, for example work, but it is more common to have perfectionism across many areas of life. Such areas can include work, study, relationships, sport and exercise, personal appearance, weight, cleanliness, personal hygiene, friendships, music, appearance of one's home, social performance: in fact, any area that is important to someone. To get started thinking about the different ways that perfectionism can impact on your life, read about the case of Aimee below.

Aimee: An example of someone with perfectionism

Aimee had perfectionism about the appearance of her home and being a good host. If Aimee was having friends over for dinner, she would spend many hours cleaning the house to what she perceived as a 'perfect' standard – and even then, she would inevitably notice some imperfections. For example, she recalled on one occasion spending six hours vacuuming, scrubbing floors, cleaning windows and doing the garden. Then she saw some streaks on the windows, and started cleaning again and again over these spots in an attempt to get the house looking perfect. Having spent so much time cleaning, Aimee ran out of time to prepare the food for dinner; when the dessert she made turned out slightly lopsided she started feeling very anxious and stressed. During the dinner, Aimee found it hard to concentrate on what her friends were saying as she was thinking about the food not being prepared to a good enough standard and was criticizing herself for this, thinking that she had 'screwed up' the dinner party and was a failure as a result.

This example shows us some of the different aspects of perfectionism. Perfectionism involves *continual striving to achieve high standards that a person has set for themselves* (e.g. 'I must have a perfectly clean house') *despite negative consequences* (e.g. feeling stressed and anxious). It also involves *self-criticism* when the person thinks they have not met one of their standards (e.g. having prepared food they perceive to be not good enough). One of the most problematic aspects of perfectionism is that people often *base their self-esteem on how well they think that they achieve these high standards* (e.g. Aimee thinking of herself as a failure for having baked an imperfect dessert for the dinner party). It is this continual striving to achieve very high personal standards, despite negative consequences, and basing your sense of self on how you measure up to those standards, that distinguishes unhelpful perfectionism from helpful perfectionism.

A definition of perfectionism for this book

In this book, when we refer to 'perfectionism', what we mean is the following:

> *Perfectionism is the setting of, and striving to meet, very demanding standards that are self-imposed and relentlessly pursued despite this causing problems. It involves basing one's self-worth almost exclusively on how well these high standards are pursued and achieved.*

People with perfectionism often feel they are unable to meet their high standards and so constantly fear failure at the same time as they continually strive to achieve. Sometimes this can result in people avoiding tasks as the fear of possible failure paralyses them. Even when they do meet their standards they will often discount this achievement, thinking that their goal was not hard enough, or that anyone could have achieved it; thus they set the bar even higher next time. In one memorable case, one of our clients, Melissa, was awarded the top mark of her year in her Media Studies exam. She dismissed this achievement by saying that the teachers had just felt sorry for her because they knew she had an eating disorder. In another example, Sophie won an ice-skating competition. Her pleasure at this achievement was fleeting and lasted no more than a few minutes. Why? Because, despite the achievement, she personally felt that she had not skated well and could have performed a lot better. Another client, Ahmed, said that he felt that there was merit in pushing himself to his limits and that he could not understand why people took the easy way out. The therapist (who invariably would take a short cut to achieve a goal if one were available) was temporarily stunned. Why would you strive and struggle if there were an alternative, easier way to achieve your goals? If your self-worth is based on striving and achievement, and you both pursue your goals relentlessly and dismiss any achievement, you are in a 'no win' situation: you're likely to feel a failure whether you actually meet your standards or not. The fear of failure is often at the heart of perfectionism.

Important parts of perfectionism

There are three main parts of perfectionism. These are:

- demanding standards and self-criticism;
- striving to meet demanding standards despite negative effects;
- basing self-evaluation on high standards.

Demanding standards and self-criticism

There is no easy way to define what a high standard is, as what may seem high to one person may not be to another. When someone has perfectionism, however, these standards are very demanding to the person themselves, i.e. difficult for that person to attain. What is important in the type of perfectionism covered by this book is that *the standards are set by you yourself and you perceive them as being demanding*. For example, earning £30,000 per year may not be demanding for some people, but may be extremely demanding for others.

Setting goals and standards that you want to achieve is a normal part of life. Perfectionism is a problem when you become very critical of yourself when you don't meet your personal standards. People with perfectionism usually focus on the negatives, and notice only the occasions when they don't meet their standards, not those when they do. It is common for them to belittle themselves over their perceived failures, repeatedly berating themselves with critical comments, for example: '*I should have done that better*' or '*I am a failure because I did not get an A in the exam*' or, more simply, '*Idiot!*'

Striving to meet demanding standards despite negative effects

Another crucial part of unhelpful perfectionism of the sort we're describing is striving to achieve demanding standards even though there are negative consequences. Examples of these negative effects are set out in Box 1.1.

BOX 1.1 COMMON NEGATIVE EFFECTS OF PERFECTIONISM

Emotional (feelings)
  Anxiety (e.g. feeling nervous, stressed)
  Depression (e.g. feeling sad, low mood)
Social
  Social isolation
Narrow interests
  Focusing almost all of one's time on a particular area (e.g. focusing mainly on work and rarely socializing)
  Limiting pleasurable activities not seen as being related to achievement (e.g. never just reading a magazine or listening to music)
Physical
  Insomnia
  Exhaustion and tiredness
  Muscle tension
  Upset stomach
Cognitive (thinking)
  Poor concentration
  Rumination (e.g. thinking about a mistake made in a task over and over)
  Increased self-criticism
  Low self-esteem

Behavioral

Repeated checking (e.g. reading an email over and over before sending it to check the text is completely accurate)

Repeating tasks (e.g. rewriting and editing something over and over)

Excessive amount of time spent on tasks (e.g. in Aimee's case taking six hours to clean the house)

Avoiding tasks

Putting off tasks (procrastination)

List-making

Being over-thorough

Hating to waste time and, as a consequence, being over-busy

What is interesting is that although some of these effects (such as being tired) are objectively unpleasant, sometimes people with perfectionism enjoy the feelings because they regard them as real evidence that they are pushing themselves to their physical limits. For example, Suzanna felt a sense of achievement when she was close to fainting with exhaustion after exercising as she felt that it was clear to her that she truly could not have pushed herself any further.

Basing self-evaluation on high standards

If you are someone with unhelpful perfectionism, you will tend to *judge your self-worth on what you do, not who you are*. Rather than viewing your idea of yourself in a balanced way, you believe that you are only a good enough person if you are achieving an excellent standard in the important areas of life. So your way of viewing yourself becomes far too dependent on the areas in which you're striving for achievement. As an example, take the case of Derek.

Derek: An example of judging self-worth on achieving high standards

Derek was a manager of sales at a large bank who based his idea of how good he was as a person on his perform-ance in two areas of his life that were very important to him: work and being a father. Derek expected nothing but exceptional performance in each of these areas. He fre-quently worked long hours to ensure that he exceeded sales targets and he was often praised by his manager for doing this. Despite this praise, Derek frequently thought that he should be doing better: he would often compare his performance to that of sales managers in other banks and think that he was not achieving as much as they were and so needed to try even harder. Derek also highly valued being a good father, and would spend as much time as possible with his children. He would often rush home from work to ensure he spent time with his children at dinner, and then go back to work for several hours after the evening meal, coming home very late and ex-hausted. He often felt he was not achieving well in either of these areas, and if one of his children was irritable with him, he would often take this as evidence that he was not spending enough time with them and was being a bad father, and would criticize himself for this. Derek often thought of himself as a failure because, despite con-stantly trying, he just couldn't seem to live up to his own expectations of being an excellent manager and father.

You can see how judging yourself as Derek did can lead to problems. Because you think you are failing to meet your standards, you think of yourself negatively overall. This leads to the negative consequences discussed above including negative emotions (e.g. anxiety, depression) and unhelpful behaviors (e.g. avoiding, procrastinating) – all as a result of basing self-worth too much on achievement of very high standards.

Different forms of perfectionism

Scientific researchers refer to different forms of perfectionism and suggest that perfectionism has a range of components. One group of researchers considers that perfectionism involves not just the pursuit of high standards for oneself, but also having high standards for other people and believing that others have high standards for you. Another group suggests that the key components of perfectionism are high personal standards and reacting to mistakes with self-criticism. Despite these differences in interpretation, all agree that for some people perfectionism is unhelpful and can clearly be separated from the healthy pursuit of excellence.

Differences between unhelpful perfectionism and the healthy pursuit of excellence

So far, you might be reading through this book and be thinking to yourself: *'Yes, but doesn't everyone try to achieve goals and standards? Isn't that just a normal part of life?'* or *'You don't get ahead by being a slacker.'* It is very important for us to be clear about the difference between perfectionism and the *healthy pursuit of excellence* or *striving for achievement*. Setting personally demanding goals and trying to achieve them can be done in a way that is positive for the individual, is associated with a sense of achievement and satisfaction, and has few negative consequences. Take for example talented musicians or elite athletes, many of whom spend a lot of time striving to achieve their demanding standards. We would not see their high standards for performance on stage or on the running track as a problem; rather, we might see this as an integral part of high achievement.

In contrast, unhelpful perfectionism of the sort described in this book involves someone's view of themselves depending on how well they think they have done in particular areas and their pursuit of their very high standards despite negative consequences. Intense self-criticism (even self-flagellation) if someone believes they have failed to meet their standards is also an integral part of unhelpful perfectionism. So if the musician were to ruminate over some trivial mistakes made when playing on stage, forget the positive aspects of their performance, perceive themselves to be a failure as a person and subsequently refuse to do anything for days on end but practice to correct those trivial mistakes, that would be unhelpful perfectionism. Or if the athlete focused on having finished second in a race, concluded they had performed poorly and were failing overall as a person and therefore needed to practice running further and harder despite injury, this would be unhelpful perfectionism. In contrast, a musician with a healthy pursuit of excellence might make mistakes in performance on stage and take reasonable measures to correct them but would still feel worthwhile as a person and be able to acknowledge the positive aspects of their performance. The athlete who finishes second in a race and thinks that they would like to do better next time and produces a reasonable running schedule that is less likely to produce injury – and still thinks they are worthwhile as a person – has the same high standards as the athlete with unhelpful perfectionism but is more balanced in their approach.

One word of caution. There is no clear-cut distinction between positive and negative striving to meet standards. Often, setting demanding standards can start out as positive but over time become negative. For example, determinedly pursuing high standards of weight loss can be helpful when a person is significantly overweight but unhelpful if the person subsequently loses too much weight. Similarly, someone can have the goal of completing all their reading lists at school, and that is appropriate; but in a different context, such as at university, it is just not realistic to expect to read everything. It is too simple to say that some people can set demanding standards and never experience negative consequences of striving, and we know that even striving to meet high standards on its own, without the self-criticism and basing your sense of self on achievement, can sometimes be associated with anxiety or, for example, problems with eating or relationships.

> *The main differences between unhelpful perfectionism and a healthy pursuit of excellence are:*
> *1 In unhelpful perfectionism the person's view of themselves is too dependent on how well they think they achieve their own demanding standards.*
> *2 In unhelpful perfectionism, people continue to pursue their standards despite negative consequences.*

For many people it is extremely difficult to see where healthy pursuit of excellence ends and unhelpful perfectionism begins. It may be that the two coexist – for example, in some areas you may be pursuing excellence in a healthy way while in another area your striving for achievement is causing significant problems and becoming unhelpful. There are some areas in which determinedly pursuing high standards is likely to be inherently unhelpful, such as trying to achieve a particular shape and weight when there is only a limited amount anyone can do to change their basic body shape. One reason why many people find perfectionism difficult to change is that it has been helpful to them in the past (as the healthy pursuit of excellence), but has become more problematic over time or is an unhelpful approach in a different situation. It is because of this complexity that it may be hard for you to see yourself as someone with unhelpful perfectionism while those around you can see it more easily.

Do I have perfectionism?

To help you determine whether you have perfectionism that might be a problem, it is useful to ask yourself the questions set out in Worksheet 1.1.

If you answered 'YES' to question 6 and the majority of the other questions, it is likely that you will benefit from using this book. Given your determination, you may well throw yourself wholeheartedly into the program and do the tasks set in Part Two to the best of your ability. This is an area where pursuing excellence can be healthy; but remember the guidance set out at the beginning of this chapter – use the book in a moderate way, setting aside some regular (but not excessive or rigid) time each week to complete your tasks. You don't have to be the best at overcoming your perfectionism – simply overcoming it will bring you joy, flexibility and freedom.

TAKE-HOME MESSAGE

- Perfectionism is defined as trying to achieve demanding standards you have set yourself, despite negative effects, and basing your self-worth on how well you think you achieve your standards.
- The main aspects of perfectionism are:
  - demanding standards and self-criticism;
  - continuing to strive to meet standards despite negative effects;
  - basing self-worth on meeting standards.
- Perfectionism is different from the pursuit of excellence and becomes a problem when your self-worth is based on meeting your standards.

WORKSHEET 1.1: QUESTIONS TO HELP DETERMINE IF YOU HAVE
UNHELPFUL PERFECTIONISM

1   Do you continually try your hardest to achieve high standards?

2   Do you focus on what you have *not* achieved rather than what you
    have achieved?

3   Do other people tell you that your standards are too high?

4   Are you very afraid of failing to meet your standards?

5   If you achieve your goal, do you tend to set the standard higher
    next time (e.g. run the race in a faster time)?

6   Do you base your self-esteem on striving and achievement?

7   Do you repeatedly check how well you are doing at meeting your
    goals?

8   Do you keep trying to meet your standards, even if this means that
    you miss out on things or if it is causing other problems?

9   Do you tend to avoid tasks or put off doing them in case you fail or
    because of the time it would take?

2

Perfectionism and other problems

Perfectionism can be associated with a range of problems. It can both cause these problems and also keep them going. These may be difficulties related to the perfectionism itself or other specific difficulties including anxiety, depression, eating problems, procrastination and obsessive compulsive disorder.

This chapter will help you to understand what types of problems are associated with perfectionism and which difficulties might relate to you.

When perfectionism causes problems in its own right

Perfectionism can cause a number of problems, as shown in Box 1.1 in the previous chapter. If you have perfectionism, you are likely to be tired (from striving all the time to achieve your goals), rather rigid and possibly isolated from other people. Perfectionism may also be causing significant problems at work. For example, if you are a teacher and you are striving for a flawless performance from your class or yourself, then this may cause friction between you and the students. Or if you are a manager, you may be responsible for giving someone their annual appraisal and, struggling for the 'right' words to say, stay up most of the night agonizing and then perceive that you perform less well than you wanted to in the appraisal itself. Maybe you and your partner are arguing over why you feel the necessity to rewash the dishes that have already been washed up. Maybe you can't send Christmas cards because the effort of personalizing each one means that they are never completed on time. Perhaps you have been forced to take a year off from your studies because you can't bear to hand in coursework that you know could be better if only you had longer to do it. Perhaps your life is ruled by 'musturbation' – I must do this, I must not do that. This is just a sample of the range of problems perfectionism can cause. At its core it is like a prison of rules and regulations, 'shoulds' and 'should nots' that govern every aspect of life. Buying this book is your first step in breaking free from this prison. It is for this reason that we have entitled the final chapter 'Freedom'.

When perfectionism is linked to other problems

Perfectionism can be associated with a range of other difficulties. Common among these are problems in the areas of anxiety, mood and eating.*

Anxiety

When a person sets themselves demanding standards and feels they might not meet those standards, this often results in anxiety. Constant thinking about, or checking on, performance can lead to feeling anxious as the person starts to fear they will not achieve their standards. It is like being constant-

---

*The criteria used to diagnose these problems can be found in the American Psychiatric Association's *Diagnostic and Statistical Manual of Mental Disorders*, 4th edn: http://www.psych.org/MainMenu/Research/DSMIV.aspx.

ly on the lookout for any sign that his/her performance may not be up to scratch; if it has slipped, the person may become very worried, anxious and stressed as a result.

Perfectionism can lead to feeling generally nervous, stressed and on edge. But perfectionism can also be associated with specific forms of anxiety, including social anxiety, obsessive compulsive disorder and obsessive compulsive personality disorder.

SOCIAL ANXIETY

Most of us can relate to feeling a little nervous when we walk into a new social situation, like a big party where we don't know many people. Social anxiety is more than just feeling shy, though: it involves a persistent anxiety about social situations, and the core part of it is worrying that you will do or say something that will embarrass you in front of others, or that others will notice that you are anxious. It also involves worrying about being the center of attention, and wishing not to be under the spotlight in social situations.

Perfectionism can both bring on social anxiety and keep it going. Often people have thoughts about the perfect way they wish to be perceived in a situation, and will berate themselves if they feel they have not met their high standards for social performance. Mark is an example of someone like this.

Mark: An example of someone with perfectionism and social anxiety

Mark was an accountant at a big firm and frequently had to attend team meetings, at which he was expected to make contributions. Mark would become very nervous and anxious before going into these meetings, fearing that he would not say things in a perfect way, or that he would be put on the spot by his boss and not have anything clever to say. He would often sweat and worry that others would notice him sweating or shaking. He would endure the meetings in great discomfort, and would spend a lot of time in the meetings going over and over in his head potential responses to questions so that he could say things in a perfect way. Often Mark would feel that he did not respond in a good way in the meetings, and that others were noticing he was anxious. He often also compared himself to other members of his team, thinking that they were smarter and had a better sense of humor than he did. When he walked away from meetings, Mark would go over everything he had said again and again, criticizing himself for not saying things in a better way, and setting his standard higher, resolving to do better next time, and aiming to appear more clever and funny at the next meeting.

We can see in Mark many of the features of social anxiety listed in Box 2.1. Being able to change your perfectionism may help diminish or banish feelings of social anxiety.

BOX 2.1 A CHECKLIST OF SOCIAL ANXIETY SYMPTOMS

- An ongoing fear of social or performance situations where the person fears they will act in a way that is embarrassing or show symptoms of anxiety.
- Entering feared social situations nearly always triggers anxiety.
- Realizing the fear is excessive.
- Feared social or performance situations are either avoided or endured with intense anxiety.

OBSESSIVE COMPULSIVE DISORDER

Perfectionism can be very closely linked to obsessive compulsive disorder (OCD). Sometimes particularly frightening and repugnant thoughts and images can repeatedly come into our minds and cause great anxiety – for example, thoughts that maybe you will accidentally harm someone or spread germs, or that something bad will happen to your family. Some people with OCD doubt whether they have performed a task 'correctly' or even whether they have performed it at all.

With OCD, when these sorts of thoughts keep occurring the person searches for a way to reduce the anxiety and perceived danger. One way people do this is to complete rituals which are aimed at reducing anxiety in the short term. For example, if a person keeps having frightening thoughts that their family will become contaminated, cleaning the home intensively can help him/her feel less anxious because he/she is 'doing something' to protect the family. In OCD these rituals (known as 'compulsions') are often based on very strict rules and must be done in exactly the same way each time. Perfectionism may play a role in the development of OCD because it is likely to influence both what a person makes of the unwanted, frightening thoughts that happen to all of us and how they respond in the compulsive or 'neutralizing' behavior. People with perfectionism and OCD often find it difficult to get to the point where they feel that the compulsions have been done *properly*, and so they get caught in a cycle of repeating the compulsions in a never-ending attempt to ensure that they have been done properly and that danger has thereby been reduced. This is a very exhausting cycle to be trapped in.

An example of someone with OCD and perfectionism is a person who feels that he/she must make sure every single detail of what they are saying, writing or reading is attended to in a perfect way otherwise something bad will happen to someone he/she loves. For example, when recalling an everyday event such a person might feel that it is essential he/she recounts every detail perfectly because if he/she doesn't then this means someone will be in an accident; and when reading he/she might need to read and reread sections over and over again to be sure they have been understood and remembered perfectly, otherwise someone will fall ill. Someone with perfectionism without OCD may like and desire order, symmetry and exactness. For someone with perfectionism and OCD, the order, symmetry and arranging are likely to be accompanied by strong feelings of 'bad luck' if they are not done properly or very strong and unpleasant feelings of something not being 'right'.

In OCD, these 'perfectionism rituals' are most often completed in order to make sure something bad doesn't happen. Negative outcomes are avoided at all costs because the person feels that if something bad does happen it will be their fault. Being over-critical with oneself and concerned about making a mistake is common in OCD. Doubts about actions are also very common both in people with OCD and in people with perfectionism, possibly because repeated checking characterizes both difficulties and we know that repeated checking causes people to distrust their memory. People with OCD tend to take on too much responsibility for things and are prone to blaming themselves. Other examples of how perfectionism and OCD can go together can be seen in the cases of Jim, Mary and Julie.

Jim, Mary and Julie: Examples of OCD and perfectionism

Jim experienced recurrent intrusive thoughts about bad luck, and feared that if he did not do his compulsions bad luck would come to his business and family. As a result Jim felt he needed to arrange things perfectly, and would set out his business cards and papers on his desk at work in a particular very precise way over and over, many times a day, to ensure good luck. He felt that if he did not do these rituals, his business might fail or one of his children might become seriously unwell.

Mary had intrusive thoughts about leaving the door unlocked and appliances left on, and feared that if she did not check these the exact correct number of times, her family would be at risk and a burglar could hurt them or the house might burn down. As a result Mary believed that she must turn the doorknob exactly four turns to the left to ensure it was locked, and must check the iron and stove were off four times each before leaving the room. If Mary felt that she had not checked exactly the right number of times, or was interrupted when she was checking, she would start the checking rituals all over again. Unfortunately Mary often started to doubt whether she had checked exactly four times, so would then restart the checking again, and it usually took her a very long time to leave the house.

Julie had hundreds of thoughts a day that she might become contaminated with HIV, for example from using public toilets, handling money in shops, or brushing past someone who she thought might be contaminated. She believed she must wash her hands repeatedly in a perfect sequence, and dry them in exactly the right way, otherwise she would become contaminated and be responsible for passing on the disease to her family. If Julie did not wash her hands exactly right, she would need to start her ritual over again and repeat it until she felt they were perfectly clean. This would result in Julie washing her hands over and over until they were cracked and bleeding. Yet despite initially feeling better for a few moments after washing her hands, she continued to worry about contracting HIV.

A checklist of OCD symptoms can be seen in Box 2.2. If you recognize that these types of symptoms are taking up a lot of your time, you might need to consider working on changing the OCD as well as your perfectionism. You could do that by reading *Overcoming Obsessive Compulsive Disorder* (see the 'References and further reading' section at the back of this book) or by contacting your GP.

> **BOX 2.2 A CHECKLIST OF OBSESSIVE COMPULSIVE DISORDER SYMPTOMS**
>
> - Repeated thoughts coming into the mind that are against the person's nature and value system and are experienced as intrusive and highly distressing. Examples are religious thoughts, unwanted or upsetting sexual thoughts, or thoughts of harming someone you care about.
> - Repeatedly doing particular things that are aimed at reducing the anxiety associated with the intrusive thoughts: for example, checking, washing, saying prayers, asking others if things are going to be OK (seeking reassurance).
> - Spending more than one hour each day on the rituals/compulsions, and finding that they cause damage in important areas like work, study or relationships.

OBSESSIVE COMPULSIVE PERSONALITY DISORDER

Obsessive compulsive disorder, or OCD, is different from obsessive compulsive personality disorder (OCPD). There is no special relationship between OCD and OCPD except that the abbreviations share three letters! Perfectionism is one of the elements by which OCPD is diagnosed. There is substantial overlap between perfectionism and OCPD, as you will see from Box 2.3, which shows you why people who have OCPD are also likely to be perfectionists.

BOX 2.3 OBSESSIVE COMPULSIVE PERSONALITY DISORDER SYMPTOMS

The overall picture is a pervasive preoccupation with orderliness, perfectionism, and control of oneself and others, at the expense of flexibility, openness and efficiency. This usually begins by early adulthood and becomes apparent in a variety of ways. OCPD is usually diagnosed if a person shows four (or more) of the following:

(a) is preoccupied with details, rules, lists, order, organization or schedules to the extent that the major point of the activity is lost;

(b) shows signs of perfectionism that interferes with completing a task (e.g. is unable to complete a project because their own overly strict standards are not met);

(c) is excessively devoted to work and productivity to the exclusion of leisure activities and friendships (not as a result of by obvious economic necessity);

(d) is over-conscientious, scrupulous and inflexible about matters of morality, ethics or values (not as a result of cultural or religious identification);

(e) is unable to get rid of worn-out or worthless objects even when they have no sentimental value;

(f) is reluctant to delegate tasks or to work with others unless they submit to exactly their own way of doing things;

(g) adopts a miserly spending style towards both self and others, viewing money as something to be hoarded for future catastrophes;

(h) shows rigidity and stubbornness.

You can have OCPD without being a perfectionist. For example, Jayne was very concerned with control and so met criteria (a) because of her orderliness, (c) because she felt that controlling her work was the key to controlling her life, (d) because she believed that if you were in control of your mind and morals, then this was fundamental to being in control in general and (e) because she felt it was wasteful to disregard items that might come in useful. She was also very miserly (g), so that when it came time to splitting the bill for an evening out with friends, she would bring out her calculator and calculate her share based on the number of glasses of alcohol she had drunk compared to other people.

If you are a perfectionist, you will almost certainly meet the criteria for OCPD. Take the example of Mark (pp. 21–2), who experienced extreme social anxiety. He prepared for his meetings by listing all the details of his projects to such an extent that he was unable to see the bigger picture of how they were progressing (a). Because of his perfectionism at work, he felt the need to triple-check all figures, and this delayed completion of the task significantly (b). He was devoted to work, partly because it afforded him some peace since when he was alone with his computers he did not have to engage in social contact (c). He was not particularly preoccupied with morality and he did not hoard, but he was unable to delegate tasks out of fear that they might not be done properly, resulting in his getting the blame and feeling as though he was a failure and lazy for not doing it every task himself in the first place (f). His need for perfection in his work and social relationships led him to be highly inflexible (h) – for example, he would not allow himself to go for a casual drink after work when asked by an attractive colleague.

If you recognize yourself in the description of OCPD and you are a perfectionist, here is the good news. Changing your perfectionism will change your OCPD. There is such overlap between the two conditions that changing one will invariably have a positive impact on the other, and you do not need to do anything more. However, if you have the form of OCPD that is without perfectionism but is interfering with your life (like Jayne in the example above), then we recommend you discuss the issues with your GP and obtain a further referral for help.

LOW MOOD AND DEPRESSION

If you have the sort of perfectionism we've been talking about, it is likely that at some point you have had feelings of being sad or down. This is not surprising, as if you spend a lot of time thinking that you have failed to meet your standards, then you are likely to end up feeling sad, low, helpless or inadequate. You may also be paralysed by indecision because of your attempts to ensure the best possible outcome.

To make the situation worse, it often happens that when you start to become lower in your mood or depressed, you lack motivation or drive to do things that you normally would do. As a result you may start to engage in some of the unhelpful behaviors we will discuss in more detail later in this chapter, such as procrastination or avoidance. This might then lead to your failing to meet your standards in consequence, which in turn might lead to an increase in depression and even more rumination (over-thinking) about how you have not met your standards. Take the case of Gemma as an example.

Gemma: An example of someone with perfectionism and depression

Gemma was a very bright student who studied hard in her undergraduate degree in literature so that she would be accepted into her Master's year. While studying for her first degree she worked very long hours, spending a lot of time editing and rewriting essays, and always trying to write the perfect assignment so she could gain the best possible mark, which she often did. Despite the amount of time this took her, Gemma always managed to submit her assignments on time. When Gemma was accepted into her Master's year and had to develop a proposal for the big research project which would determine her overall grade at the end of the year, she became very preoccupied with wanting to develop a perfect project. She felt the outcome was hugely important: if she did not write the perfect proposal, she believed, then she would not complete a good project, and if she did not do this then she might not be awarded her master's degree, which had always been her most important goal. As a result, Gemma started procrastinating, putting off getting started on writing her proposal; when she tried to think of ideas she often found herself staring at a blank computer screen. Gemma started becoming tearful, thinking to herself, 'I will never be able to develop a good project,' and her mood began to plummet. This was despite meeting with her supervisor and discussing ideas together. Gemma started to sleep in late into the morning as she felt so tired, and then when she did get up she felt she had no motivation, and became tearful again, feeling guilty for not having made progress on her proposal. She became reclusive and stopped seeing her friends, and started to eat less as she did not feel hungry. This pattern went on for several weeks until she missed the deadline for her proposal.

We can see in Gemma's case how perfectionism can lead to symptoms of depression, and how, as the more depressed she became, the more she ruminated on not meeting her standards. In this way it is easy to get stuck in a vicious cycle between perfectionism and depression.

While this book can certainly help you to overcome your perfectionism, it is important to note that if you have been feeling five or more of the symptoms in Box 2.4 *every day for more than two weeks*, then you may be depressed. In this case it would be useful for you to read *Overcoming Depression* by Paul Gilbert (see the 'References and further reading' section at the end of this book) or consult a mental health professional or doctor. If you can tackle your depression, this will give you a better chance of successfully working on your perfectionism. If you are feeling as though life is not worth living, you should seek professional help immediately from your GP or a mental health practitioner.

> ### BOX 2.4 A CHECKLIST OF SYMPTOMS OF DEPRESSION
>
> - Feeling sad and down most of the time.
> - Not being interested in things you used to like doing.
> - A distinct increase or decrease in your weight or appetite.
> - A noticeable increase or decrease in your regular amount of sleep.
> - Feeling tired and low on energy.
> - Feeling very guilty or not worthwhile as a person.
> - Poor concentration.
> - Thoughts or plans of wanting to hurt yourself or thinking life is not worth living.

Eating difficulties

It is very common, particularly in women, for perfectionism to go hand in hand with eating difficulties. Perfectionism is a risk factor for eating difficulties, which means that if someone is a perfectionist, then he/she is more likely to develop an eating disorder than someone who is not. If you have eating difficulties, then one main area where your perfectionism is likely to be expressed is in the area of eating, your body shape, your weight and the need for control. Think back to the previous chapter when we were discussing areas of life where your perfectionism might be expressed: your shape and weight is another one of these areas. Take the example of Ifioma.

Ifioma: An example of someone with perfectionism and bulimia

Ifioma was an attractive young woman whose weight was in a healthy range. However, she felt very unhappy with the way she looked and thought she was fat and needed to lose weight so that she would be more attractive. Ifioma was always dieting as she felt she needed to lose ten pounds: this would bring her to her goal weight, which she thought would be perfect for her. Ifioma had many rules about her eating, including not eating more than 1,000 calories a day, not eating carbohydrates after lunchtime, and not eating a range of foods that she saw as fattening, which included chocolate, chips, sweets, butter, ice cream, cheese, biscuits, white bread, nuts and cakes. Ifioma would often be able to maintain 'control' over her eating during the day, and would eat very little for breakfast and lunch, but as the day continued she became hungrier and would belittle herself for this, thinking that she was already fat and telling herself to stop thinking about food. If Ifioma had a stressful day at work or an argument with her boyfriend then she would think she deserved just one treat to help her relax, and might eat a chocolate bar on the way home from work or her boyfriend's house. This immediately triggered guilt in Ifioma for breaking her dietary rules, which would lead her to drive to the shops to buy some of the foods she avoided like ice cream and cakes. She would eat large quantities of these foods very quickly and had a sense of loss of control over her eating. After eating the food she would vomit to try to get rid of the calories. This left Ifioma feeling terrible, and afterwards she would berate herself for having broken her rules and become even more determined to restrict how much she ate the next day so that she could lose weight. This left Ifioma in a vicious cycle of striving to keep stringent dietary rules and then binge-eating and vomiting, which she did up to five times a week.

We can see how perfectionism is linked with Ifioma's eating problems. She holds very rigid rules and demanding standards in regards to her weight and what and how she eats. When Ifioma breaks one of these rules, she feels that she has failed to meet her standards with regard to dieting and weight loss and she is then likely to binge. This is called 'all or nothing thinking', and we will discuss this in detail in Part Two (Section 7.5), as it is one of the most common aspects of perfectionism.

Ifioma had bulimia nervosa, a term which you have probably heard, along with the more familiar anorexia nervosa. The main difference between these eating difficulties is the actual weight of the person. The two problems have much in common and a checklist of symptoms can be seen in Box 2.5. If you recognize your own symptoms here, and particularly if your weight is low (Body Mass Index below 17.5)* or you are regularly vomiting, then you should consult a psychologist, other mental health professional or doctor as you might need more assistance; these eating difficulties can result in some serious physical effects. Alternatively, we recommend you read a self-help book such as *Overcoming Bulimia Nervosa and Binge-Eating* by P.J. Cooper or *Overcoming Binge Eating* by C.G. Fairburn (see the 'References and further reading' section at the end of this book).

---

* Body Mass Index is calculated by dividing your weight (in kilogrammes) by the square of your height (in metres).

> ## BOX 2.5 A CHECKLIST OF SYMPTOMS ASSOCIATED WITH EATING DIFFICULTIES
>
> - Judging self-worth largely on eating, shape and weight, or their control.
> - Recurrent binge-eating, which involves a sense of loss of control over eating and eating a large quantity of food.
> - Extreme efforts to control weight. These may include vomiting, using laxatives or diuretics, dietary restraint (e.g. going all day without eating) or excessive exercising.

What to tackle first: Perfectionism or the disorder?

If you are someone with perfectionism and other difficulties such as those described above, it is important to work out the relationship between them. For many people, it is possible to overcome the anxiety disorder, depression or eating problem without ever tackling the perfectionism and vice versa. For others, it may be that the perfectionism is contributing to the other difficulties. A useful idea developed by Christopher Fairburn, an internationally renowned expert on eating difficulties, is that of a house of cards.* If you want to bring down the house, you need to take out the main cards at the bottom that are supporting all the others. If you are someone whose perfectionism is contributing to your other difficulties, then tackling perfectionism will have a beneficial effect on the anxiety, depression or eating problem. It can also be useful to think of difficulties such as anxiety, depression and eating problems like the leaves of a weed and perfectionism as the root. If you pull at the root, and try to dislodge it from the ground, then the leaves are likely to start to wither.

---

*In his book *Cognitive Behaviour Therapy and Eating Disorders*: for details, see the 'References and further reading' section at the end of this book.

Unhelpful behavior

Perfectionism is not only linked with anxiety, depression and eating difficulties; it can also cause behaviors which are unhelpful and cause problems. It's easy to see, for example, how someone with perfectionism, trying continually to meet the demanding standards they set themselves, might start to use avoidance behaviors. Another of the most common behaviors that someone with perfectionism may use is procrastination. (We were going to tell you about that now but we think we'll leave it for later . . .)

Seriously, though, these and other behaviors that can both result from perfectionism and keep it going are serious problems. We outline them here and are also discuss them in more depth in Chapter 4, where we look at the factors that keep perfectionism going. In general, what lies behind these unhelpful behaviors is the aim of trying to reduce what is perceived as poor performance.

Avoidance

Avoidance can be defined as *something that is done by a person with an attempt to decrease or escape from anxiety about a particular situation.*

One of the most common reasons for avoidance in people who have perfectionism is a fear of failure. This is often based on negative predictions they make about a situation in which they feel under pressure to perform. Examples of negative predictions and the avoidance behavior that results can be seen in Box 2.6.

BOX 2.6 EXAMPLES OF AVOIDANCE BEHAVIOR AS A RESULT OF NEGATIVE PREDICTIONS ABOUT NOT MEETING STANDARDS

Negative predictions	Avoidance behavior
'I will fail the exam'	Do not sit the exam
'I will not get a podium finish'	Do not compete in the race
'I will not host a good dinner party'	Never invite friends for dinner
'I will not look good tonight'	Do not go out to a party
'I will not have a perfectly clean house'	Never invite friends around for coffee
'I will not play my music perfectly'	Never play violin in front of people
'I will never get a promotion'	Do not approach boss about career prospects
'I will have gained weight'	Do not weigh self

As you can see from Box 2.6, all these negative predictions are based on expecting the worst. Someone with perfectionism fears the worst possible outcome in their performance, and so, rather than risk being faced with that poor performance, chooses to avoid the possibility of it happening. While this is usually done with the aim of trying to avoid failure, in fact avoidance behavior can have the opposite effect, as it is likely to cause the person not to achieve in reality, the very thing they are afraid of and in fact trying to prevent. For example, if a student does not turn up to their exam, then they may indeed fail the unit they were studying. If a person engages in a lot of avoidance behavior through repeatedly avoiding testing their performance, they may never have a chance to find out that in fact their performance may be better than they fear. Avoidance also means you don't get a chance to practice a task, learn from mistakes and continue to improve as a result.

Another motive for avoidance is that the task to be completed is so huge and awful, because of the high standards, need for thoroughness and 'all or nothing thinking', that it becomes unpleasant. If brushing your teeth takes you an hour, it becomes easier not to brush your teeth at all than to spend an hour brushing them. If tidying your child's bedroom means you have to vacuum, clean behind the bed and clear out the cupboards, then again it is easier to allow the mess to mount up. Although many people with perfectionism live in immaculately kept homes, many also live in a mess because their goals for tidiness cannot be achieved, the task is too enormous and so they have given up altogether.

Procrastination

Procrastination – delaying a task until a later time – is very common among people with perfectionism. Procrastination often occurs because someone is so preoccupied with having to complete a task perfectly that they prefer to delay starting the task rather than face doing it less than perfectly – so it is in fact a kind of avoidance. As with other avoidance behaviors, it often stems from a fear of failure so intense that the person would rather put off starting a task than risk failing to perform it to the high standard they have set themselves.

Some of the common thoughts behind procrastination can be seen in Box 2.7. Ask yourself some of these questions to help detect whether they identify some of the thoughts that go through your mind when you procrastinate.

> **BOX 2.7 QUESTIONS TO HELP DETECT THOUGHTS ABOUT PROCRASTINATION**
>
> - Do you think it will take such a long time to complete a task that you would rather put it off as you know it will take too long?
> - Do you leave things until the last minute (e.g. write an assignment the night before it is due) so that you will have an excuse if you do not do well?
> - Would you rather delay starting a task than face not doing well at it?
> - Do you delay getting started on a task because you think you will feel very anxious or overwhelmed when doing it?

There are of course many other thoughts that may cause someone to procrastinate. The problem with procrastination in people with perfectionism is that this behavior is done with the aim of achieving a perfect performance, and yet, like the avoidance behaviors discussed above, it is likely to have the opposite effect. Continually delaying getting started on a task is likely to heighten anxiety to a degree where it may possibly impair performance once the task is started – or might mean that there is simply not enough time left to produce a good performance when the task is finally embarked on (for example, writing an assignment the night before it is due rather than giving oneself a week to write it). Procrastination can also lead to an accumulation of tasks, so that when one actually has to start doing something, the prospect of just starting can seem overwhelming. Take the case of Simon as an example.

Simon: An example of someone with perfectionism and procrastination

Simon had perfectionism about the cleanliness, order and appearance of his home. He thought that he had to have everything perfectly ordered, neat and tidy in every room of his house. However, Simon would often procrastinate and put off cleaning his house, as he would not know where to start. He would find himself moving from room to room, staring at untidy areas and thinking that he needed to organize each room perfectly and spend a long time cleaning each area in order for his house to be organized and look good. Simon often became overwhelmed with how much time it was going to take to clean and organize to a perfect standard, and so avoided starting at all. Gradually his house became more untidy and messy, which resulted in him feeling even more overwhelmed and procrastinating further.

You can see from the example of Simon that procrastination in fact has the opposite effect to that intended (guarding against poor performance), in that the more one procrastinates, the less likely one is to meet the required standards (in Simon's case a perfectly clean and ordered house).

Performance checking

Many people with perfectionism repeatedly check how their performance is going (we refer to this as 'performance checking behavior'). Box 2.8 sets out some examples of areas in which perfectionism is expressed and the type of performance checking behavior someone might do in that area.

BOX 2.8 EXAMPLES OF PERFORMANCE CHECKING BEHAVIORS IN DIFFERENT AREAS OF PERFECTIONISM

Perfectionism area	Performance checking behavior
Weight and shape	Repeated weighing, staring in mirror, checking body for fat
Work	Comparing work output at end of each day that of other team members
Friendships	Checking how often a friend calls you compared to other friends
Sport	Repeatedly comparing race finish times with those of other athletes
Study	Repeatedly asking teacher or tutor for more feedback and if performance is OK
Dating	Checking how often one is asked on a date compared to friends
Social	Checking after each sentence how what you said sounded to others by looking at the expressions on their faces
Entertaining	Repeatedly asking dinner guests if the food is OK

We can see from the examples in Box 2.8 that performance checking behavior can take different forms. These include:

- *testing* our performance – for example, by redoing a task;
- *comparing* ourselves to others;
- *seeking reassurance* from other people about how well we have carried out a task.

However, performance checking behaviors rarely result in a person feeling satisfied with their performance. Instead, it is likely that when we compare ourselves to others we think we have not performed as well as them. Often in perfectionism people choose unrealistic people to compare themselves to. For example, a novice athlete might compare himself to a professional, a woman might compare her body shape to that of a model in a fashion magazine, or a worker might compare his performance to that of his most senior colleague. As a result, comparing ourselves with others usually makes us feel worse about ourselves; this in turn makes us even more likely to compare our performance to that of others and keeps perfectionism going.

Seeking reassurance is also unlikely to result in a person feeling good about their performance. This is because people may not give a response that makes the person feel reassured, and even if they do, the feeling of reassurance is likely to be only fleeting, after which worry about performance usually kicks back even more strongly than before.

Counterproductive behavior

Many people develop habits that are designed to alleviate their symptoms of anxiety, depression, eating difficulties or perfectionism, only to find that unfortunately their strategies backfire and are counterproductive. For example, if someone suffers from anxiety attacks, they might always sit near an exit row in a cinema and take water and anxiety medication with them. This can be counterproductive as it increases the person's thoughts about and preoccupation with danger, and they also don't find out that they don't have an anxiety attack if they sit elsewhere. Similarly, if someone has social anxiety, they might always keep their arms by their sides to guard against others noticing they are sweating, or never eat spicy food in case it results in their face becoming red and others thinking they are blushing due to anxiety. This behavior would be counterproductive because people may think this person is somewhat peculiar, thus responding in a way that increases the social anxiety. The basic problem with this kind of behavior is that the person never has a chance to find out that the very thing that they are worried about (e.g. others noticing blushing, having a panic attack in the cinema) might not occur – and that if it does, it will not be a catastrophe.

Counterproductive behavior in perfectionism covers things we do with regard to performance as a way of making us feel more at ease about performance, or even as a way of making up for what we see as a mistake. A common behavior in perfectionism is list-making. For example, you may make multiple lists of what you need to achieve for the week at work so that you don't miss anything out, which would impair your performance. The purpose behind this behavior is to guard against the object of anxiety – in this case, falling short of the standard of perfect performance at work. Another example is organizing: for example, someone may ensure that several times a day at work they file each paper perfectly in the section where it belongs, and always try never to have loose papers on their desk, as a result of worrying about losing documents and being seen as incompetent. Both constant list-making and organizing can be counterproductive by consuming large amounts of time that would otherwise be spent on the tasks at hand. Working through the night to prepare for a presentation is another common behavior that can easily backfire, as it often leads to a worse performance the next day as a result of tiredness. Being over-thorough, trying to do too many things at once (multi-tasking) and rushing to avoid wasting time are all common counterproductive behaviors in perfectionism that are tackled in Part Two of this book.

TAKE-HOME MESSAGE

- Perfectionism is linked to anxiety. General feelings of anxiety about performance are common; also, specific anxiety problems such as social anxiety and OCD can occur with perfectionism.
- Perfectionism is linked to depression, which can result when someone often thinks they are failing to meet their standards.
- Perfectionism is linked to eating difficulties. It is a particularly important factor that puts someone at risk of eating difficulties and keeps such difficulties going.
- Perfectionism can result in unhelpful behavior. This includes avoidance behavior, performance checking, procrastination and counterproductive behaviors.

3

What causes perfectionism?

This chapter is for background and general interest, and is more technical than the other chapters. If you wish to skip this chapter and just read the 'Take-home message' at the end and then move on to Chapter 4, that is fine.

Both genes and environment

Like any personality style or temperament, perfectionism results from both our genes and our environment. Studies of twins suggest that between 24 per cent and 49 per cent of perfectionism may be inherited, that is, passed down in the genes from earlier generations of the family. So the genes we inherit from our parents can influence the development of perfectionism; but the figures above suggest that our environment plays a greater role. Even if genes were the main contributor to the development of perfectionism, this would not mean that perfectionism could not be changed. Irrespective of your genetic inheritance, the decisions you make, and the actions that you take, can help you to change the unhelpful influence of perfectionism in your life.

Again, we know that perfectionism, like any other complex human behavior, will result from many different factors that are all interconnected, not from one single cause. There are likely to be numerous genes that have a small or moderate effect on perfectionism that involve several biological pathways in interaction with various environmental variables. In addition, other aspects of temperament are likely to moderate the impact of perfectionism in your life. For example, some people may have a strong desire to attain high standards but may also have very healthy self-esteem, and thus they do not get overly critical of themselves on the occasions when they do not attain some of the standards that they have set themselves.

It is important to understand that there are multiple causes of perfectionism. This means that there are a number of different approaches that can be effective in decreasing the harmful impact of perfectionism in your life, and that there won't be just one way of tackling your perfectionism. This process of decreasing the harmful influence of perfectionism in your life can be likened to trying out a number of tools – some will not be useful, and can be discarded; others will be helpful and can be added to the toolbox. The type and number of tools that you use will vary depending on the situation you're trying to tackle.

Specific risk factors for perfectionism

While we know that both genes and environment are involved in giving rise to perfectionism, we know very little about which specific genes or which specific environments contribute to it. Most research to date has focused on what high levels of unhelpful perfectionism can cause, and not vice versa. We know that there is an association between the levels of perfectionism that people report and their reports of perceived pressure to be perfect from other people in their lives. Basically this tells us that the more of a perfectionist a person is, the more likely they are to perceive that other people expect perfection from them, and the more likely they are to believe that other people in their lives will criticize them for not achieving perfection. What we cannot tell from these associations, however, is whether people with a high level of perfectionism believe that everyone around them has the same standards that they have, or whether being exposed to people with high standards can cause perfectionism in an individual.

Some people with perfectionism have perfectionist parents and/or come from families with excessively high standards; others do not. It may be that, whatever the reason behind the beginning of perfectionism, perfectionist behavior is rewarded by other people and may be rewarding for the person who practices it, thus strengthening such tendencies, as depicted in our example of Suzie below. Being a perfectionist can mean that a person appears to be reliable, in control, thorough and responsible, and it can give that person a sense of control and order and structure. However, as we noted in Chapter 1, over time perfectionist behavior leads to negative consequences, such as fatigue, self-doubt, procrastination, lack of concentration, lower self-esteem, depression and anxiety.

Suzie: An example of how perfectionism developed and was maintained

Suzie's parents were both teachers and they encouraged Suzie and her elder sister to attain high standards at school. They expected nothing but the best, and were disappointed when Suzie achieved only As rather than A+s for her schoolwork. Suzie also recalls her parents requiring her and her sister to be better behaved in social situations than any other children present. Any small lapses in good behavior in public brought forth emotional reactions (tears, shouting and stony silences) after the family had reached the privacy of their own home. Suzie grew up to fear these scenes and indeed any expressed disapproval, and made it her main goal in life to achieve high standards so that she wouldn't feel guilty about being a bad person. In secondary school Suzie received a lot of positive feedback from her teachers about her responsible behavior and academic achievements. She enjoyed this attention, as she did not feel that she was very good at making and keeping friends. Suzie is now 32 years old; she lives independently from her family, but has regular contact with them that is enjoyable and supportive. However, over time she has increased the pressure on herself to attain high standards, and feels a failure in her work as a physiotherapist if her clients are not absolutely satisfied with the service that she gives them. In order to prevent any mistakes from happening in her work with her clients, Suzie spends hours writing up the case notes for each client, and often works late in order to achieve this. As she spends more time on the notes, she is becoming increasingly anxious, in case she misses any detail that might lead her to not offer the best service to her clients.

What does it all mean for treatment?

As you can see from what has been written so far in this chapter, we do not really have any very specific idea of all the different things that can cause perfectionism and their relative importance. The bottom line, however, is this: we do know that, no matter what causes perfectionism, unhelpful perfectionism can be reduced, thereby significantly improving the quality of people's lives. In other words, you do not have to understand how your perfectionism started in order to overcome it.

How do we know this? There have been several evaluations of therapeutic approaches designed to decrease unhelpful perfectionism that have shown certain approaches to be effective. The first was an evaluation of a self-help book, *When Perfect Isn't Good Enough*.* Two treatment groups were set up. One received the book and worked through it over the course of eight 50-minute weekly meetings with a postgraduate psychology student (not a trained therapist). The second group received the book, instructions and a timetable on how to use the book, and minimal contact with the postgraduate psychology student – just two brief phone calls over the eight-week period. Each group was followed up three months after the eight-week treatment period ended. One indicator of outcome was how many people had experienced clinically significant decreases in perfectionism by the follow-up – 'clinically significant' meaning not just a large decrease but one likely to be reported by the person as making life better for them. As you can see from Figure 3.1, around 50 per cent of people in the group that met with the student had clinically significant reductions in both types of perfectionism that were measured: concern over mistakes and personal standards. Fewer people reported clinically significant reductions in the group that received only the book, but 40 per cent of the group did report experiencing clinically significant improvement in concern over mistakes.

In addition to decreases in perfectionism, there were improvements across a number of other areas. For example, for those people who worked through the book with the postgraduate student, clinically significant improvements were experienced in obsessionality by 29 per cent of the group, in

---

*This evaluation was carried out by Jessica Pleva and Tracey Wade in Australia in 2007. For full details of the book evaluated (Anthony and Swinson, 2009), see 'References and further reading'.

depression by 38 per cent of the group, and in feelings of being responsible for things that go wrong by 54 per cent.

So what can we conclude from this study? The first conclusion is that relatively brief periods of treatment with non-specialist therapists can be effective for reducing perfectionism and the other types of problems that accompany it, such as depression. The second is that it is probably best to get some sort of therapeutic support as you work through this book, in order to make the most of the ideas that are contained here. This sort of support should be available via your GP, through self-referral as part of the government's 'Improving Access to Psychological Therapies' service (www.iapt.nhs.uk) or privately (see www.babcp.com for a therapist who is accredited by the British Association of Behavioural and Cognitive Psychotherapy).

The second evaluation of a perfectionism treatment comes from the work of Roz Shafran and her colleagues at Oxford University. They compared people going through ten sessions of therapy for perfectionism to people who were on the waiting list for therapy, and therefore not currently receiving it. People receiving therapy experienced clinically significantly greater reductions in perfectionism than the people waiting for therapy. Of all the people who then went on to do therapy, 75 per cent experienced clinically significant decreases in perfectionism, and these treatment gains were maintained at follow-up 16 weeks after the end of treatment. As in the previous treatment study, treating perfectionism also had beneficial effects in other areas of the participants' lives. Of those people who entered treatment, 50 per cent met criteria for an anxiety disorder or major depressive episode immediately prior to treatment; by the 16-week follow-up stage this had fallen to 20 per cent. Similar positive results with treatment resulting in decreases in perfectionism and symptoms have also been found in studies

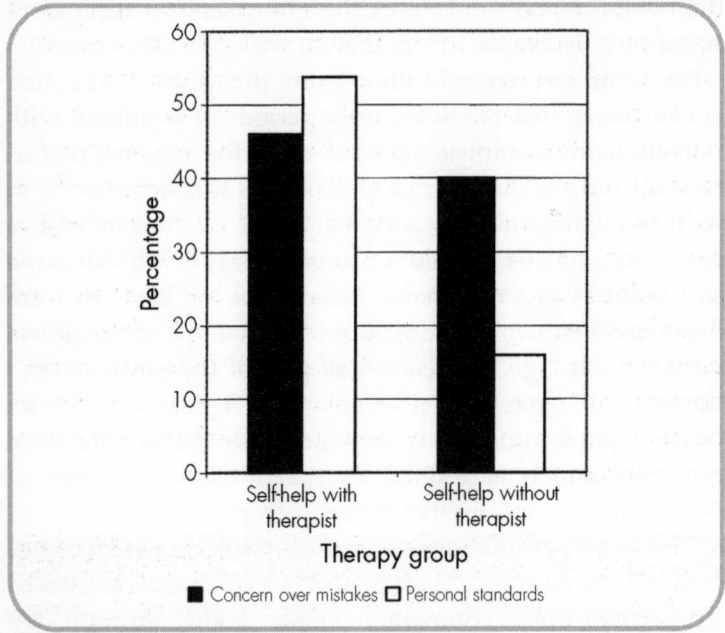

Figure 3.1 Clinically significant decreases in perfectionism after a brief treatment with a non-specialist therapist

by Roz Shafran and Dominic Glover in the UK, and Sarah Egan and Paula Hine in Australia.

This idea that treating unhelpful perfectionism has benefits for other areas of people's lives was reinforced by the results of a treatment study by Anna Steele and Tracey Wade in Australia. They offered people who had bulimia nervosa eight brief sessions of therapy with a postgraduate psychology student (again, not a trained therapist). Three different treatments were compared: a treatment for perfectionism, a treatment for bulimia nervosa, and a mindfulness treatment. All three groups improved significantly over time with respect to their bulimia nervosa. At six-month follow-up, these improvements had been maintained, and people receiving the perfectionism treatment had also experienced significant decreases in depression and concern over mistakes, as well as a significant increase in self-esteem.

The research on treatment of perfectionism tells us that starting treatment for perfectionism can have something of an avalanche effect in a person's life. Beginning work on reducing unhelpful perfectionism also starts to have helpful effects on related problems in a person's life, such as low self-esteem, depression, anxiety, obsessionality and disordered eating. This occurs even though these other problems are not explicitly targeted. This is because perfectionism can have unhelpful effects in a person's life, as discussed in Chapter 2, and so winding back the perfectionism reduces these as well.

TAKE-HOME MESSAGE

- Apart from knowing that both genes and the environment contribute to the development of unhelpful perfectionism, we do not know what specific events or influences cause perfectionism.
- We don't need to know the causes of perfectionism in order to be able to significantly decrease unhelpful perfectionism.
- Decreasing unhelpful perfectionism also leads to improvements in other problem areas of a person's life, such as low self-esteem, depression, anxiety, over-thinking and disordered eating.

4

Why perfectionism persists

Chapter 2 described a long list of difficulties associated with perfectionism, including problems with work, studying, socializing and feelings of low mood, anxiety and fatigue. If perfectionism were all negative, it would be relatively easy to change. We know, on the contrary, that perfectionism can be difficult to change – and an important reason for this is that it can serve many positive functions at the same time as causing so many problems.

Positive aspects to perfectionism

Aamina: Why be average if you can be the best?

Aamina, aged 45, is a highly attractive successful businesswoman. She runs her own company and is widely admired. She has won numerous awards for her innovative approach to business and for encouraging women in the workplace. Her personal motto is 'Nothing's impossible, if you try.' Although she has been in a number of relationships, she generally found these unsatisfactory as her partners typically wanted to spend more time with her than she felt able to give without it affecting her work negatively. She earns a six-figure salary, has a high-flying lifestyle and enjoys many aspects of her work. At night, however, she is plagued by thoughts about all that she has not done at work, and how her company could have been bigger and better if only she had acted differently. She feels a fraud for winning the awards, perceiving that she could have done more than she had and to a higher standard. She feels that her work has been superficial and lacks meaning as she is not helping the world's poor. She acknowledges that nothing she achieves will ever be good enough for her, and is fearful of a life of hard work without any sense of personal satisfaction. She feels a 'fraud' and fears failure intensely.

It is clear that although Aamina's perfectionism is causing her real problems, it would be extremely difficult for her to change. There are practical reasons for her to keep working – her lifestyle depends on a high income and jeopardizing that would pose great challenges. Also, she is likely to think that changing her perfectionism would have a negative impact on her success at work – and yet, although this sounds as if it would obviously be the case, in fact it isn't obvious at all. This book is about testing such assumptions – in Aamina's case, finding out exactly what would happen if she were less perfectionist and more flexible. Could she have her cake (her success) and eat it too (flexibility)? She has little else in her life apart from her work and so it would be very difficult to change anything that she might regard as potentially causing her difficulties in this area. Her hard work and objective success are socially reinforced by admiration from her colleagues and the public acknowledgment of awards. Although she may dismiss these in the privacy of her own mind at night, they are also very difficult for her to give up.

Many people with perfectionism fear mediocrity. They regard themselves as achieving what they do because they strive. Many will say, '*I do OK not because I'm clever but because I work hard.*' Many believe that they are less able than others but that they can compensate and hide this by working hard. This may be true; *but it may not* and it is absolutely, fundamentally important to find out what the real situation is and what would happen if changes were made.

Despite the anguish that such striving can bring, the thought of not striving and potentially achieving less brings more anguish since the self-worth of perfectionists is so dependent on pushing themselves as hard as possible and doing well. People with perfectionism are caught between a rock and a hard place – the perfectionism is causing many problems but it is bringing with it the rewards that come with striving and pursuing high standards. These rewards are often social and include prizes and praise. Reports from school often rate the effort that children put into their projects in addition to performance. The mother who manages to look immaculate while also maintaining an immaculate home is frequently the object of admiration at the school gates, attracting comments such as *'I don't know how she does it.'* Working hard is socially condoned; the opposite end of the spectrum – laziness – is not. However, there is a middle ground.

In addition to the social rewards, there are financial rewards for working hard and success in the work arena; and there are positive internal rewards as well. On the one hand, perfectionism brings with it social isolation and takes up a huge amount of time. On the other, it can serve the function of avoidance for those who may not enjoy socializing and who recoil from company. Keeping a perfect home, practising a musical instrument, training hard – all mean that the person doesn't have time to socialize with others or to engage in other tasks that they may not find valuable or enjoyable. Being focused on one task can give a sense of control and predictability and, particularly in the case of perfectionism and eating disorders, a sense of order in one's life.

The positive aspects of perfectionism are shown in Box 4.1 overleaf. Not all people will experience every positive aspect, but the range of positive rewards illustrates why perfectionism can be so difficult to change.

The cognitive behavioral model of perfectionism

In 2001 we spent a great deal of time trying to work out the nature of perfectionism and why it persists. Why couldn't people just weigh up the advantages and disadvantages of being a perfectionist, decide that the disadvantages outweighed the advantages and change? The answer is: it isn't as simple as that. It isn't a straightforward evaluation of pros and cons, leading to the logical conclusion that change is necessary and the making of that change. Part of the reason why it is difficult to change is that the perfectionist person's self-evaluation is overly dependent on striving and achievement. Another part of the reason is the strengths of the positive benefits described above. Yet another part of the reason is fear – fear of failure, fear of change and fear of discovery.

We do not underestimate how hard it can be to change; but we also know how hard it is *not* to change, to go on being a perfectionist. This book is about encouraging you to find out what happens if you make small changes – does the worst happen or do you get some pleasant surprises? Take the example of Leung, who discovered that if he ate regularly and slept regularly rather than working through mealtimes and sleeping only when he felt he had completed enough work in the evening, his grades actually improved. He found out that his previous belief that he wasn't naturally clever so needed to work hard was an over-simplification of the real situation. He did better if he put some effort into the task, but he didn't do *even* better if he went over the top with his work.

BOX 4.1: SOME OF THE REWARDS OF PERFECTIONISM

Reward	Description	Example
Socially condoned	People are praised and rewarded for working hard and having high standards	'She's amazing – I don't know how she does it – family, work, tidy home. She's really superwoman'
Gives structure	Each day is focused on achievement	'He starts work at 7 a.m., has a half-hour lunch break and doesn't come home until 8 p.m., by which time the kids are already in bed'
Gives sense of control	Each day is predictable	'I start by vacuuming the house from top to bottom and tidying away as I go. I know that everything is in its place and I can go about the day's business then'
Brings achievements	Hard work brings achievement and recognition from colleagues such as 'employee of the month'	One of the criteria for being selected by McDonald's to go to the Beijing Olympics was 'hard work'
Avoidance of feared people/ situations	Spending time striving for achievement leaves little time for socializing or being in new situations that may provoke anxiety	'I won't leave the children with a babysitter because that's not "being a good mum" so I never go out to parties unless my parents can babysit'
Avoidance of discovering feared aspects of self	Many people fear that they only do well because they work hard and that such work compensates for a innate lack of ability	'I've done really well but it's only because I train so hard – harder than all the other athletes. I'm sure I would do much worse if I didn't put in so much effort. I don't have real natural talent like some of the others'

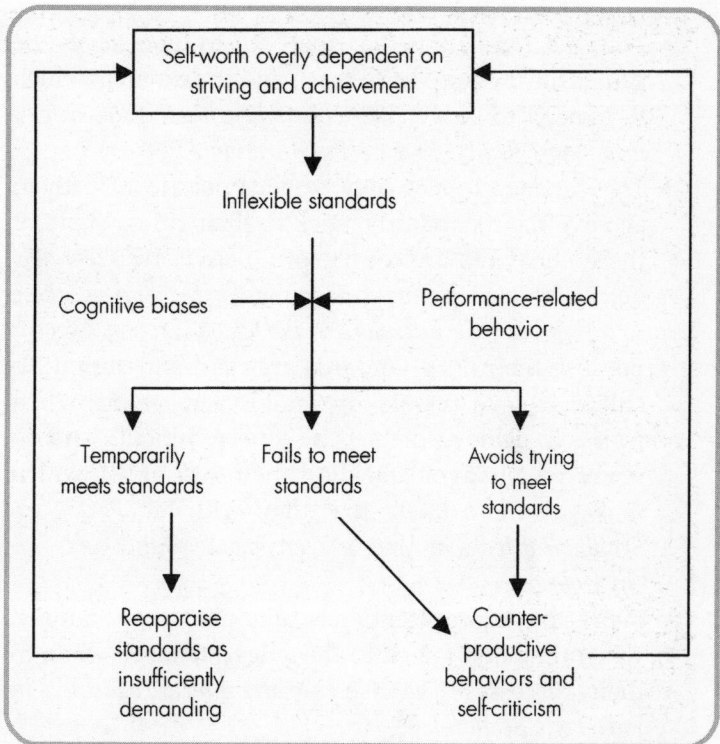

Figure 4.1   Why perfectionism persists

There are other important reasons why change is so difficult and why perfectionism persists. Various processes lock people into the cycle of perfectionism, and these are self-perpetuating and hard to break. We put them into a diagram to help people understand why perfectionism persists. The diagram is adapted according to the particular needs of each individual, but a general framework is shown in Figure 4.1. This focuses on the way of thinking, feeling and behaving that keep perfectionism going.

We suggest that people get locked into perfectionism for the following reasons:

- They set rigid rules that spell out to themselves the standards they expect to reach and the extent to which they need to strive. *We look at how these rules can be made more flexible in Part Two, Section 7.5.*
- They engage in a variety of behaviors to help them achieve their standards/stick to their rules. Many of these behaviors are counterproductive. *We show how behavioral experiments can be used to address these counterproductive behaviors in Part Two, Section 7.4.*
- Because the rules/standards are rigid and very difficult to achieve, people often fail to achieve them. Just trying to achieve them is also very difficult, and so many people avoid tackling their task at all, which makes it more likely that they will fail. *Part Two, Section 7.8 looks at how to overcome avoidance and procrastination.*
- People pay more attention to their perceived 'failures' when they don't stick to the rules/standards than to their 'successes'. *These biases of attention are addressed in Part Two, Section 7.6.*
- People react to the perceived failure to achieve their standards/stick to their rules with lowered mood and self-criticism. They over-generalize the perceived failure at one task into an overall failure of themselves as a person. This ties up their self-evaluation to achievement even more strongly. *These thinking biases are addressed in Part Two, Chapters 8 and 9.*
- Even when people stick to their rules or reach their standards, they discount their achievements, saying the task was 'too easy', and remake the rules so they are even harder to achieve. This suggestion has been supported by recent research in which college students performed a task with a goal and received

feedback on success. Following the feedback, they were asked to choose (a) the same goal or (b) a more difficult goal for the next task. The greater the perfectionism, the more likely the participants were to choose a more difficult goal. This type of strategy is a guaranteed way to make yourself feel a failure. *In Part Two, Sections 7.3 and 7.7, we investigate what 'normal' standards might be and suggest how you can use a technique called 'cognitive restructuring' to help.*

Implications for treatment

The cognitive behavioral model of perfectionism is a starting point for understanding what is keeping perfectionism going. The rules, behaviors and thinking biases that characterize perfectionism and keep you locked into a cycle are all interrelated. This means that if you make a change in one area, you will automatically see changes in other areas too. The first step to changing your perfectionism is understanding what is keeping it going and personalizing the model to reflect your own situation. Chapter 5 and Section 7.1 will help you do this.

TAKE-HOME MESSAGE

- People with perfectionism are locked into a self-perpetuating cycle characterized by a range of ways of thinking and behaving.
- It is difficult to change because perfectionism is often reinforced socially and because of the ways of thinking and behaving that are part of perfectionism.
- The cognitive behavioral model is used as a 'template' for discovering what is likely to be keeping you locked into a cycle of perfectionism.

PART TWO

Overcoming Perfectionism: Learning to Change

5

The first steps

Strange as it may seem, it is not necessary to understand the cause of a problem for it to be addressed successfully. For example, a surgeon can mend a broken leg without knowing whether the person broke it falling from a ladder, falling down the stairs or dancing. It is the same with mental health problems. The treatments that have had the most success are those that tackle what is keeping the problem going in the here-and-now, rather than those that look backwards in search of causes. Of course, later on it is important to take a step back and think about factors that may have contributed to the onset of perfectionism so that you can be mindful of them and try not to go back into old perfectionist ways, and we looked at some of the possibilities in Chapter 3. However, the most important first step is to understand what is keeping the problem going.

At the time of writing, the most successful approach to tackling perfectionism has been cognitive behavioral therapy (CBT). In Chapter 3 we briefly outlined some research studies that have shown that such an approach can help reduce perfectionism. It does so by tackling the thoughts, feelings and behaviors that keep the problem going. Cognitive behavioral therapy is also the most successful type of therapy in treating problems such as depression, anxiety and eating disorders, so it is not altogether surprising that a similar approach can help to address perfectionism.

Your goals

Do you want to overcome perfectionism? If not, then fair enough. It's tough enough to change when you do want to and almost impossible to change if you don't. It's perhaps more likely that, despite having read about the problems that can be associated with perfectionism, and understanding some of the negative effects it can have, you might find this a difficult question to answer. One of the issues that comes up when we talk with people in therapy about overcoming their perfectionism is anxiety about whether the therapist is in fact asking them to give up or lower their standards – and when you have perfectionism, the idea of lowering standards in some way is a very scary idea. Take a look at Box 5.1 and some of the examples of concerns you might have about the idea of lowering your standards.

BOX 5.1 EXAMPLE CONCERNS ABOUT LOWERING STANDARDS

- If I lower my standards, I will let myself completely slip and not perform at all
- If I lower my standards, I will become lazy (I don't want to be a slacker!)
- If I lower my standards, others will think I have let myself go
- If I lower my standards, others will not praise me for doing well any more
- If I lower my standards, this will result in me losing something I value (e.g. job)
- If I lower my standards, I will be overwhelmed with anxiety
- If I lower my standards, I will not achieve
- If I lower my standards, I will not progress in life
- If I lower my standards, I will be average (like you – yuk)

> *This book is NOT about lowering standards but is about addressing the over-dependence of your self-worth on striving and achievement. It is about giving you a choice of how to live your life, considering what is best for you and those around you.*

We have already seen in Chapter 4 that there can be both advantages and disadvantages to perfectionism, and it can seem frightening to contemplate losing any of the advantages that striving gives you. But we know that striving to meet standards in itself does not have to be a negative thing; remember the discussion in Chapter 1 about the difference between unhelpful perfectionism and the healthy pursuit of excellence. So it is important to be very clear here that when we are talking about overcoming perfectionism, it is not with the aim of trying to get rid of striving for standards. Instead, the goal is to reduce the dependence of your self-esteem on striving and achievement so that you can choose *which* standards to pursue and decide which are perhaps better treated as general guidelines rather than rigid rules. Perversely, it may be that you actually *achieve more* when you make some changes and increase your flexibility; we cannot guarantee that, but we know that learning how to overcome your perfectionism can in fact help you to become more effective. Often it is the case that when you have perfectionism you are striving so hard and pushing yourself to such a degree that your performance can become poorer because of fatigue and because you are working so intensively towards your goals. So overcoming perfectionism can in fact help you to become more effective, and enhance your performance. No promises, though!

What is keeping your perfectionism going?

Chapters 3 and 4 described some factors that we have found typically contribute to perfectionism, and Figure 4.1 suggested how they may link together. The first step to treating your perfectionism is to personalize this model and adapt it so that it fits in with your own experiences – to draw your own 'perfectionism cycle'. We'll start with an example, using the case of Guptha described below.

Understanding Guptha's perfectionism

Guptha, aged 59, was a married father with three children. He had not been outstanding at school but had always worked hard. After leaving school at 16 he had got a job with an aeroplane manufacturer, and had worked there ever since. Now, nearing the end of his career, he was fairly senior. He had always worked extremely hard and had prided himself on rarely making an error. He got on well with his colleagues, although they complained about his perfectionism because it slowed things down at work as Guptha felt he needed to consider all possible options carefully and in great detail before making any decisions. He put a similar degree of care into bringing up his children – he was cautious about allowing them to take any risks – and was constantly seeking reassurance that he was a good father. Being a good father and good at work was of fundamental importance to the way Guptha viewed himself as a person. He had a great number of rules in place to ensure that he did not make mistakes. His rules included 'I must consider all options carefully before making any decisions, however small,' 'I must do everything I can to protect my children from harm' and 'I should always do my best.' Yet although other people considered him a successful father and a success at his job, Guptha felt a failure in his work. He would repeatedly go over in his head the times when he had not considered all possible options, or would think about what would have happened if he had made a different (better) decision. He often dug his nails into his hands and called himself a 'loser' and a 'prat'. When things were really bad, he avoided being with his children in the belief that he would do more harm than good by not being a good enough father.

Guptha's difficulties can be viewed within the framework of the cognitive behavioral model described in Chapter 4. It might look something like Figure 5.1.

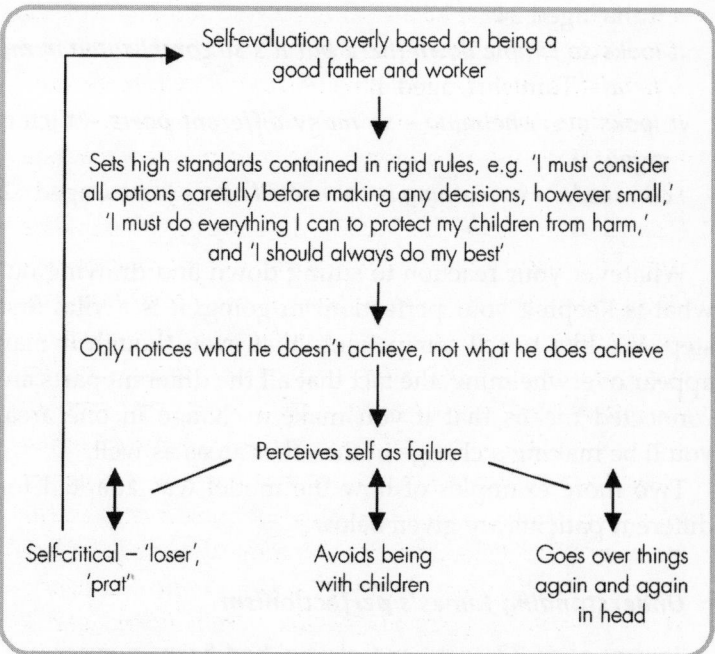

Figure 5.1   What is keeping Guptha's perfectionism going?

In cognitive behavioral therapy for perfectionism, the first step is always to understand what is keeping the problem going by drawing a diagram such as the one above. This diagram is not necessarily the real 'truth'; rather, it is a collection of ideas about the main features of perfectionism and how they fit together. As you work your way through this book over a period of time, your own version of the diagram will evolve, with different features being added and adapted.

When people see the features that maintain their difficulties drawn out in this way, they respond in a variety of ways. Here are a few examples:

> *It feels more manageable now that it is down on paper –* Talia, aged 24
>
> *It looks so simple down there but it's so complicated in my head –* Tanushri, aged 47
>
> *It looks overwhelming – so many different parts –* Victor, aged 31
>
> *I can see how everything is connected now –* James, aged 32

Whatever your reaction to sitting down and drawing out what is keeping your perfectionism going, it is a vital first step. We like to tell our patients that even though it may appear overwhelming, the fact that all the different parts are connected means that if you make a change in one area, you'll be making a change in the other areas as well.

Two more examples of how the model was adapted for different patients are given below.

Understanding James's perfectionism

James, aged 32, was, and always had been, a procrastinator. He always put off tasks until the very last minute, though he almost always did the task in the end. He wasn't overly distressed by his procrastination, although he acknowledged that it was very frustrating for those around him. No matter how small the task – for example, replying to a wedding invitation – James would only do it at the very last minute. He was clear about his reasons for procrastinating: he believed that if he started the task earlier, then he would check he had done it properly and go over it repeatedly right until the deadline anyway. Doing things at the last minute was a way for him to cope with his perfectionism. However, though he believed that 'if a job was worth doing, it was worth doing well', because he always left things to the last minute he often did not do well in tasks or made silly mistakes (e.g. returning the wedding invitation without a stamp). He was in a role at work which placed few demands on him as he did not want the pressure and stress of having to achieve. Although part of him felt that he was not living up to his potential, another was realistic in acknowledging that it would cause him too much stress to take on a more responsible role.

A diagram that James might draw to show how the features of his perfectionism are related and what is keeping the problem going is shown in Figure 5.2.

Understanding Catherine's perfectionism

Catherine was a 20-year-old ex-student of Cambridge University. She was having a year away from her studies because she was finding it difficult to cope with the workload. She had always got top marks in her studies and had won prizes for horse-riding as well. Whatever she set her mind to, she achieved. She derived some pleasure

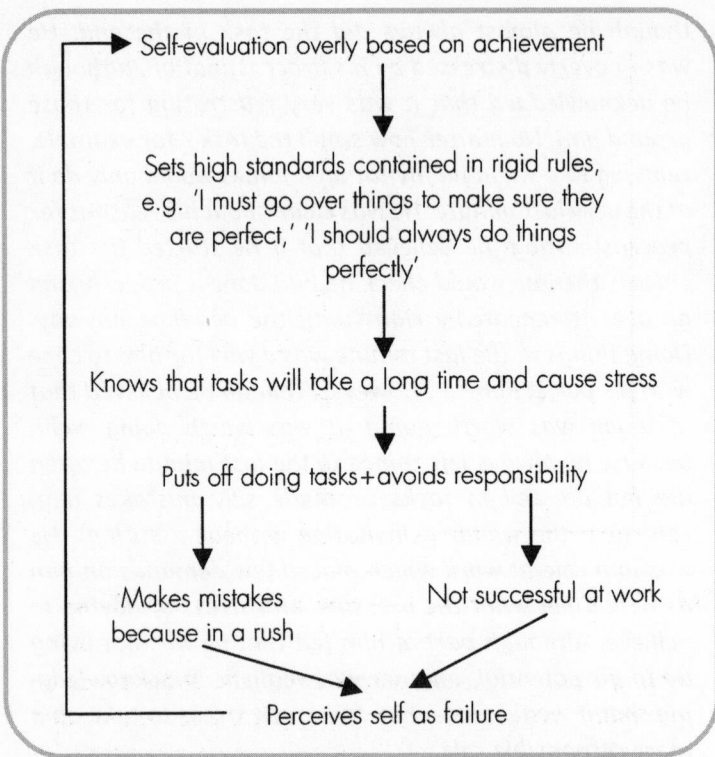

Figure 5.2 What is keeping James's perfectionism going?

from her achievements but it was usually short-lived as she went over situations in her head and found fault with herself. Her primary difficulty with university was that she was unable to complete all the reading that was required for her course. At school, she had worked most nights and weekends and had managed to get the work done although it had meant she rarely went to parties and had few friends. At university, despite working as hard as possible, she could not complete the reading list. Her university had tried to help her by telling her that she did not need to read everything, but she felt unable to start

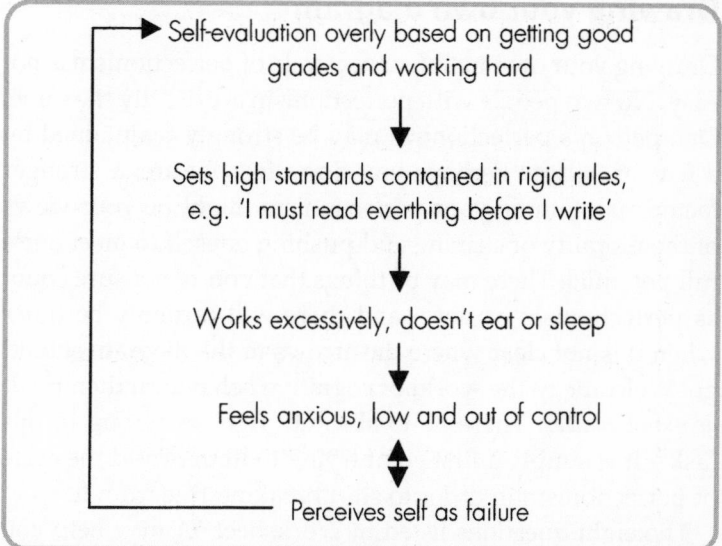

Self-evaluation overly based on getting good grades and working hard

↓

Sets high standards contained in rigid rules, e.g. 'I must read everthing before I write'

↓

Works excessively, doesn't eat or sleep

↓

Feels anxious, low and out of control

↕

Perceives self as failure

Figure 5.3   What is keeping Catherine's perfectionism going?

writing until her reading was complete. After three or four months of problems with eating and not sleeping due to work, she went to her GP for some tablets to help with her low mood, anxiety and feelings that she was out of control in her life.

A diagram that shows how Catherine's perfectionism is maintained is shown in Figure 5.3.

It is important to make the point that for Catherine, as for many of us, the strategy of pursuing high standards has been helpful at some point. Catherine won prizes for her horse-riding and won herself a place at one of the best universities in the world. However, the strategy for dealing with her work (reading everything and focusing on work to the exclusion of all else) backfired when she went to university as she was unable to adjust her standards and rules.

Drawing your own diagram

Drawing your own maintenance cycle of perfectionism is not easy. No two people with perfectionism are exactly the same. One person's perfectionism may be strongly maintained by a fear of failure. Perhaps you don't fear failure; a stronger factor maintaining your perfectionism might be your views of the morality of striving and pushing oneself to meet one's full potential. There may be things that you're not sure count as perfectionism or not – and there will certainly be times when it is not clear where the arrows in the diagram should go! Welcome to the world of cognitive behavioral therapy. *It does not matter.* There is no absolute right or wrong in this task – it is simply a first go at trying to understand the cycle of perfectionism in order to start breaking free from it.

The eight questions listed in Worksheet 5.1 may help you to make a start on your own diagram. Find a blank piece of paper you can draw your diagram on, and follow through the questions, using the examples you have already read to help and guide you.

Having drawn your diagram of what is keeping your perfectionism going, take a moment to think about your reactions to it. Does it make sense to you? How do you feel? What are your views about change? It is likely that you'll feel ambivalent about change, and this is addressed in the next chapter, which will discuss the pros and cons of change for you. However, be assured that change is possible, and can have great rewards: our patients liken it to being freed from their own internal prison of rules, regulations, failure and stress. We wish to encourage you to have a go, and we firmly believe that the greatest motivation for change is change itself. Once you try to do things differently, you will gain freedom and flexibility, and the interconnections between the various aspects of your problem mean that such changes

WORKSHEET 5.1: QUESTIONS TO HELP YOU DRAW YOUR DIAGRAM OF WHAT IS KEEPING YOUR PERFECTIONISM GOING

Q1. Is how you think about yourself, feel about yourself or judge yourself dependent on achievement or striving? Is it too dependent? Would you feel bad about yourself *as a person* if you did not achieve or strive to achieve high standards? If so, this is likely to be a factor in keeping your perfectionism going, and it can be put at the top of the diagram.

Q2. Do you have excessively high standards? If so, this needs to be in the diagram, and as these demanding standards are likely to stem from how you judge yourself on the basis of striving and achievement, it might go underneath the first point above, connected by a downward arrow.

Q3. Do you have rules to help you achieve your high standards? If so, list some of the most obvious ones and put those into the diagram below 'high standards'.

Q4. Does 'all or nothing thinking' mean that you feel you often don't meet your standards and that you perceive yourself as a failure as a result? If so, put this into the diagram with a recent example.

Q5. Do you react to the perceived failure with self-criticism? If so, this should be in the diagram too, again with examples.

Q6. Put examples of 'counterproductive' behavior such as avoidance, procrastination, repeated checking, being overly detailed or overly thorough, and multi-tasking into your diagram and think about what leads to these. Is it failure to meet your standards? Is it self-criticism? Is it anxiety, low mood or stress? Put in the answers you come up with.

Q7. Think about how anxiety, low mood and stress contribute to the cycle of perfectionism. Add these to the diagram.

Q8. If you do perceive that you sometimes meet your standards, put this in the diagram (as in Figure 4.1), with a recent example. Think about how you react to such success, how long those feelings last and whether you discount your successes. All these features should be in your diagram.

spread rapidly. Of course, it's not easy – but nor is living with perfectionism.

TAKE-HOME MESSAGE

- By focusing on what is keeping your perfectionism going, you will be able to begin to make changes.
- Drawing the different elements in the cycle that keeps your perfectionism going is the first step in knowing what changes need to be made.
- There is no 'right' or 'wrong' understanding of your perfectionism and what keeps it going. As long as your diagram makes sense to you, that's all that matters.

6

The costs of changing

The fact that you are reading this book means that part of you is considering changing your perfectionism, presumably with the goal of keeping the good aspects but reducing the damaging impact it currently has on your life. Even though change can mean improving your life, it's not easy to decide to change long-held habits and patterns of behavior. These habits and patterns emerged for a reason and may still perform some useful functions, or achieve certain goals in your life. However, these habits and patterns are also having damaging consequences in your life, some of which were outlined in Chapter 2. Thus people approach the idea of change with mixed feelings – being caught between fearing the consequences of change and wanting the benefits of change. The purpose of this chapter is to help you explore these mixed emotions and count the cost of change before you embark on this process.

Are you are ready for change?

The first thing to ask yourself is: how important is it to you to change the way perfectionism impacts on your life? You can find this out by completing the first part of Worksheet 6.1. If it turns out that it is not very important for you to make changes, you may need to ask yourself if this is the right time to start working on your perfectionism.

The second thing to ask yourself is: how confident are you that you can change the way perfectionism impacts on your life? The second part of Worksheet 6.1 will help you to answer this question. Sometimes it can be very important for someone to make changes, but if they lack confidence in their ability to make these changes, it can hold them back from experimenting with change.

The importance of change

Take some more time to think through why it is important for you to change. Think about the pros and cons of keeping things as they are and allowing the current impact of perfectionism on your life to continue by completing Worksheet 6.2.

First, list the advantages of keeping things the same in the box headed 'Advantages of not changing my perfectionism'. Second, think of the advantages of changing your perfectionism and write these down under the heading in the lower left-hand box. Now, think of the question the other way around. What would be the disadvantages of not changing your perfectionism and what would be the disadvantages of your perfectionism continuing as it is now? Write these down under the appropriate headings in the right-hand pair of boxes.

It may help to reread Chapter 2 of this book as you do this exercise, in order to make sure you have captured all the disadvantages in your life.

Don't worry if you found it difficult to complete Worksheet 6.2. Sometimes people find it hard to think of the advantages and disadvantages of change when they have been living with an unhelpful behavior for so long. It can help to think of the questions from other perspectives – for example, by looking at the situation through someone else's

WORKSHEET 6.1: CONSIDERING THE IMPORTANCE OF CHANGING
PERFECTIONISM AND YOUR CONFIDENCE THAT YOU CAN MAKE CHANGES

First think of the importance of changing perfectionism as being a ruler marked from
0 to 10, as shown below, where 0 equals not important at all and 10 equals
extremely important. What score would you give yourself out of 10? Put a circle
round the appropriate number.

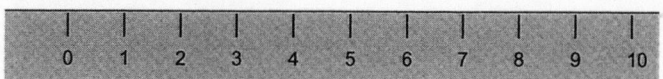

Now ask yourself the following questions:
(1) If the score isn't 0, why not? What are the reasons that change is more
important to you than 0?

(2) If the score is not 10, why not? What would have to happen to make this score
higher? What would you be noticing about yourself if the score was to be
higher? What resources would you have to draw upon to get to the higher
score? What people in your life may be able to help you get there?

Now think of the ruler as indicating your level of confidence in being able to
change, where 0 equals no confidence at all and 10 equals extremely confident.
Decide what score you would you give yourself out of 10 and circle that number.

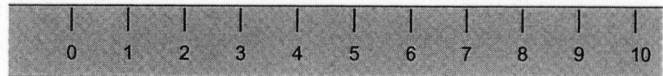

Now ask yourself the following questions:
(3) If the score isn't 0, why not? What are the reasons that your confidence in your
ability to change is greater than 0?

(4) If the score is not 10, why not? What would have to happen to make this score
higher? What would you be noticing about yourself if the score was to be
higher? What resources would you have to draw upon to get to the higher
score? What people in your life may be able to help you get there?

WORKSHEET 6.2: PROS AND CONS OF CHANGING PERFECTIONISM

Advantages of not changing my perfectionism	Disadvantages of not changing my perfectionism
Advantages of changing my perfectionism	Disadvantages of changing my perfectionism

eyes. Choose a person who is close to you and cares for you – now go back to the boxes, and consider each of the headings again from this person's eyes. What advantages and disadvantages would they see for you in staying the same or making changes? Add these thoughts to the boxes. If it helps, it may be useful actually to ask the person these questions. Sometimes you will be surprised at what others notice about the destructive influences of perfectionism on your life.

Another perspective that can help when thinking about the pros and cons is considering what your life might be like in the future without change, and with change. It can feel difficult to make changes in the present; perhaps you feel it would be better to wait for 'a better time'. However, if you consider what the future will look like if you don't change, this can sometimes make beginning to change look more urgent. Look at the first box in Worksheet 6.3 and consider what will be happening in the various areas of your life one year from now if there is not a change in the perfectionism in your life. Write down the ideas as they come to you. Now do the same for the next box, thinking about how these areas in your life will look if the impact of perfectionism in your life is reduced.

Now, when considering everything you have written in the three worksheets so far, answer the following questions:

- What scares you the most about reducing perfectionism in your life?
- What are the most compelling reasons for reducing perfectionism in your life?

WORKSHEET 6.3: CONSIDERING THE LONG-TERM COSTS AND BENEFITS
OF PERFECTIONISM

In one year's time . . . still having perfectionism	
Area of life	*What will have happened in this area?*
My social life	
My work/education	
My finances	
My emotional health	
My relationship with my partner	
My relationships with my children	
My relationships with close friends	
My relationships with my parents/siblings	
My contribution to the community	
My spiritual life	
Other (please specify)	
In one year's time . . . no longer having perfectionism	
Area of life	*What will have happened in this area?*
My social life	
My work/education	
My finances	
My emotional health	
My relationship with my partner	
My relationships with my children	
My relationships with close friends	
My relationships with my parents/siblings	
My contribution to the community	
My spiritual life	
Other (please specify)	

Confidence in your ability to change

The major fear that may hold some people back from working to change their perfectionism is that they fear their lives will not function as well without it. If you have been judging your worth according to your ability to meet high standards, then you may feel that the process of change will leave you feeling utterly lost, like trying to navigate through the Amazon jungle without a guide or a compass. Impossible. How will you know if you are worthwhile? How will you judge yourself as a person? Your confidence in being able to run your life without perfectionism may be low. Consider the example of Gloria below and see if any of these issues apply to you.

Gloria: What perfectionism was achieving in her life

Gloria is a second-year university student and has always had high standards for her academic achievement. This caused her problems in her final year at school, as she was reluctant to hand in anything that she did not consider 'perfect'. This reluctance stemmed from worrying about what her teacher would think about her if the work was not excellent. She feared that the teacher might respect her less and consider her to be a student who was not worthwhile spending time on. Gloria also felt that she was letting herself down if she produced less than excellent work, and that she would become a second-rate person if she started handing in only 'good enough' pieces of work. Fortunately at this time she was able to discuss these fears with the teacher, and the teacher was able to help her hand in work that Gloria considered was not yet excellent enough for marking. Gloria always achieved high marks for these pieces of work, even though she considered them to be unpolished and unfinished products. However, when Gloria started attending university, she encountered these same problems but felt unable to talk to others about them. She stopped participating in tutorials or attending workshops, as she worried that other people would consider her input unsatisfactory and think she was a failure as a person. The same issues started to cause problems for Gloria in her part-time work as an administrative assistant. She feared that less than perfect work would show people how hopeless she was as a person and so she avoided completing certain tasks. Even though the costs of perfectionism mean that Gloria is failing at university and also in danger of losing her part-time job, Gloria herself still fears that she might become a second-rate person if she changes her perfectionism in the areas of study and work.

One way of increasing your confidence about changing and not relying on always attaining high standards in order to feel good about yourself is to think about identifying yourself as a person who has something to offer across many life areas rather than just one or two. You may also like to consider who it is you want to *be* in these areas, as opposed to what you want to *achieve*. In Worksheet 6.4 you can see the same areas of life you considered earlier. Consider who it is you want to be and what you want to do in each of these areas. In what ways will your life look different if you start to enrich all these areas rather than spending so much of your time pursuing excellence in just one or two?

One great advantage of spreading how you judge yourself as a person across many areas of your life is that you are no longer 'putting all your eggs into one basket'. If you are judging yourself on just a few areas of your life, then if things are not going well in these areas you will be judging yourself

WORKSHEET 6.4: BEING THE PERSON YOU WANT TO BE ACROSS DIFFERENT AREAS OF YOUR LIFE

Area of life	Who do you want to be in this area? What do you want to do in this area?
My social life	
My work/education	
My finances	
My emotional health	
My relationship with my partner	
My relationships with my children	
My relationships with close friends	
My relationships with my parents/siblings	
My contribution to the community	
My spiritual life	
My valued pastimes and hobbies	
My fitness and physical and nutritional health	
Other (please specify)	

harshly as a person. If you are putting your eggs in a few different baskets, then when things do not go right in one area, the chances are that something will be going fine in another area, or that you are satisfied with your life in another area.

You can use the information you have set down in Worksheet 6.4 to step back and see the whole picture of who you are as a person, rather than judging yourself on that one bit of work or that one performance that you considered was not up to scratch.

You have done a lot of thinking as part of working through this chapter. Now for one last thing! Go back to the 'importance' and 'confidence' rulers at the start of the chapter (Worksheet 6.1). Think about where you would put yourself now. Have your ratings changed at all? If so, reflect on what has happened to make you change these ratings. It may be useful to discuss this with another person who you feel is an important support in your life.

Even if you still have some doubts, we encourage you to give the ideas in this book a wholehearted try. You will soon be aware of change, and will see the freedom and flexibility you will gain without a big decrease in performance. Once you see that these changes are helpful and improve your quality of life, you are in a position to decide if you want to continue with further change.

TAKE-HOME MESSAGE

- Changing perfectionism is not easy because even though there are advantages to change, there can also be fears and disadvantages.
- Sometimes the biggest obstacle to experimenting with change is the fear of becoming a 'second-rate' person if you do not achieve high standards in some areas of your life.
- It can help to step back, see your life as a whole, and consider the person you want to be, and what it is you want to do, across all the areas in your life.

7

Specific techniques to overcome perfectionism

We haven't yet discussed indecision, but if you have perfectionism you are probably plagued by indecision because you are so heavily invested in striving and achievement. Some degree of indecision is normal (see Section 7.3 on 'Surveys') – in fact, we were plagued by indecision about how to structure this next part of the book! What we have done is to divide this chapter into nine 'subchapters' – a sequence of sections that set out different tools in your toolkit for tackling perfectionism. They all have the same goal: to build up information about what the reality of your situation is. How hard do you need to work to achieve your standards? What is your emotional reaction to failure to achieve? How do other people view the same task? What actually happens if you do X or don't do Y?

The first task is to identify the problem areas (Section 7.1). The second is to arm yourself with the information you need to tackle your perfectionism (Section 7.2). Sections 7.3 through to 7.8 provide the basic tools in the 'toolkit' and are the methods you need to use to help you change (plasters or band-aids are provided throughout!). All the various tools are compatible with the others, and you will probably need a combination of several of them.

7.1 Getting started: Identifying problem areas

The first step in overcoming perfectionism is to identify the areas of your life in which it is a problem. This will involve monitoring your perfectionism through completing the worksheets in this chapter. This will help you to understand how perfectionism is affecting your life, and will serve as the basis for understanding the particular areas you need to target in overcoming perfectionism.

In therapy, people often do not like the idea of keeping a diary of their problems at first. They say that it will take too much time, or they will not remember to record everything, or it might be overwhelming to be confronted with their problems, or they might feel embarrassed recording those problems. While these concerns are understandable, in fact we find that once someone starts keeping records they find it is not overly time-consuming (provided they keep the sheets in a prominent place, such as a handbag or briefcase), they do remember to complete them, and they are able to cope with recording their problems without excessive shame or embarrassment. One of the reasons why it is so important to start recording your problems is this: we know that the process of recording a particular problem behavior – that simple act of writing it down – can itself help to reduce the behavior. This is because monitoring and recording our problems can help us to understand them and gives us a sense of direction about how to overcome them.

Identifying your areas of perfectionism

It is possible to apply high standards to any area of your life. To help you identify the areas in which your perfectionism is a particular problem, read through the examples in Box 7.1.1.

BOX 7.1.1 EXAMPLE AREAS OF PERFECTIONISM AND TYPICAL THOUGHTS AND BEHAVIORS

Area of perfectionism	Thoughts	Behaviors
Eating	I must not eat high-fat food	Restrict eating
Shape	I should be a size 6 to look good	Restrict eating, increase exercise
Weight	50 kg is the perfect weight for me	Restrict eating, increase exercise
Social performance	I must appear funny and clever	Rehearse jokes and stories
Checking locks, appliances	I must be 100 per cent sure	Check and re-check
Ordering objects	Things must be in perfect order	Order and arrange objects daily
Organization	Lists are necessary to be organized	Write extensive lists
House cleanliness	My house must always be clean	Excessive cleaning
Appearance	My appearance must be perfect	Always wear make-up and creaseless clothes
Hygiene	I must have perfectly clean hands	Wash hands over and over
Artistic performance	I need to produce superior art	Re-do paintings
Musical performance	I must not play a note wrong	Avoid playing concert
Sporting performance	To perform my best I need to train harder	Train more than coach recommends
Academic performance	I must always achieve above 80 per cent	Spend many hours editing assignment

Work performance	I have to be excellent at work	Work 12-hour days
Intimate relationships	I must find the perfect partner	Date numerous people, regularly break up due to perceived flaws
Parenting	Good mums care for their kids	Do not allow children to be babysat
Health and fitness	I must exercise every day	Engage in self-criticism when do not exercise daily
Entertaining	A good host makes perfect food	Spend entire weekend planning and preparing a meal

Now that you have read through some examples, use Worksheet 7.1.1 to make some notes about the areas in which, in the past month, you think you might have applied high standards. The key to helping you identify these is to reflect on areas where you think you must excel, where you must always have things just right, or where you would feel very worried if you were to perform at a lower level. The worksheet involves following three steps: first identifying the areas that apply to you, and then reflecting on your thoughts and behaviors in each of these areas. If you have perfectionism in an area not listed, attach a blank sheet of paper and follow the same process. Then reflect on what you have written and answer the question at the end of the worksheet.

Completing this worksheet can help you to understand more about your areas of perfectionism. Were you surprised to see that perfectionism affects many areas of your life? Were there other areas not listed that you thought might also be affected by it?

WORKSHEET 7.1.1: WHICH AREAS OF PERFECTIONISM APPLY TO ME?

Step 1: Circle each area in which you think you have perfectionism
Step 2: What goes through your mind about this area (thoughts)?
Step 3: What do you do in response to perfectionism in this area (behaviors)?

Area of perfectionism	Thoughts	Behaviors
Eating		
Shape		
Weight		
Social performance		
Checking locks, appliances		
Ordering objects		
Organization		
House cleanliness		
Appearance		
Hygiene		
Artistic performance		
Musical performance		
Sporting performance		
Academic performance		
Work performance		
Intimate relationships		
Parenting		
Health and fitness		
Entertaining		

Reflection on Worksheet 7.1.1
What did you learn about your perfectionism by completing this worksheet?

Monitoring your areas of perfectionism

Now that you have identified areas where you have perfectionism, the next step is to monitor them. This will include recording the times when you are perfectionist; other things you might record include setting high standards in a particular area, or criticizing yourself for not meeting standards. Consider the general points about self-monitoring in Box 7.1.2 before you start self-monitoring.

BOX 7.1.2 GENERAL POINTS ABOUT SELF-MONITORING

- Self-monitoring is the first step in overcoming perfectionism, and can be a tool to help you change.
- Self-monitoring works best if you record the situation at the time, rather than after the event.
- Self-monitoring can help you to gain perspective on your perfectionism and become more objective, because writing things down helps us get distance from our problems.
- It is normal to feel hesitant before doing self-monitoring for the first time; however, it is often easier than you think, and not as overwhelming as you might predict it to be.
- It is useful to keep self-monitoring sheets somewhere close at hand (e.g. handbag, briefcase) to make it easier for you to record events, thoughts and feelings at the time.
- Think about all the obstacles that might get in your way and prevent you from self-monitoring. They might be practical (e.g. not having a pen with you) or emotional (it is too difficult to face up to the problem and writing it down might make it feel worse). How might you overcome these difficulties? (We'll have some suggestions on this later.)

Why is it important to monitor your perfectionism?

We know from the treatment of anxiety, depression and eating problems that self-monitoring is an extremely important part of changing. It does lots of different things. For a start, it enables you to realize the true extent of your difficulties. Often people with perfectionism are surprised about how much of their life is taken over by perfectionism-related thoughts, emotions or behaviors. It also enables you to distance yourself from those thoughts, feelings and behaviors associated with perfectionism. Obtaining such distance, and being able to view your thoughts, feelings and behaviors more objectively, without drowning in the quicksand of your perfectionism, begins to free you up to make change. Another important function of self-monitoring is that it enables you to detect patterns in your perfectionism and, ultimately, to stop and think about some of the things that you do concerning perfectionism that you currently just do automatically.

Overcoming problems with self-monitoring

Think of practical ways you can overcome any barriers to monitoring. For example, you could set aside a particular time each day to review your records, or set a reminder in your diary or mobile phone to record your monitoring sheets during the day. The basic monitoring sheet is set out in Worksheet 7.1.2, with an example of how you might fill it in. Emotional difficulties with self-monitoring are challenging, but it is never too early to grasp the fundamental principle associated with changing your perfectionism – *test your beliefs*. You might think that you will be very upset by seeing your perfectionism written down on paper. Does that happen? Are you as upset as you thought you would be? How long does your distress last? Motivate yourself by reminding yourself of the reasons why you want to break free from your rules and rigidity, and the advantages inherent in trying things another way. Use this book flexibly – for example, combine a behavioral experiment (see Section 7.4) with self-monitoring.

Did you notice patterns in your perfectionism? For example, did the same areas of perfectionism appear throughout the week, or did you note a range of areas? Were there similar thoughts and behaviors you engaged in over the week? And what was the effect of your perfectionism thoughts and behaviors on your feelings? Did you notice that the thoughts and behaviors were leading to negative feelings? It is likely that simply by beginning this general monitoring of your areas of perfectionism you will have started to identify your particular difficulties with perfectionism. Just keeping records of your areas of perfectionism as in Worksheet 7.1.2 is a very good step towards understanding the problem.

Monitoring of specific perfectionism behaviors

In addition to this general monitoring, you might also find it useful to keep a record of your specific behaviors associated with perfectionism.

In Chapter 2 we outlined how perfectionism can lead to avoidance, procrastination, performance checking and counterproductive behaviors. It is important to monitor and understand these behaviors as they are a core part of what keeps perfectionism going. So understanding your own patterns of specific perfectionism behaviors is an important step in overcoming your problem. For more detailed information on the specific behavior, refer back to Chapter 2. A summary of the definitions of these behaviors is provided in Box 7.1.3.

WORKSHEET 7.1.2: SELF-MONITORING AREAS OF PERFECTIONISM

Over the next week, identify examples of when your perfectionism is a problem.
Step 1: Record both the *area of perfectionism* and *the particular situation*.
Step 2: Record your thoughts. Ask yourself: 'What was going through my mind?'
Rate how strongly you believe the thought: 0 per cent=do not believe at all;
100 per cent=completely believe.
Step 3: Record your behaviors. What did you do?
Step 4: Record your feelings. Examples are: anxious, sad, angry, ashamed,
depressed, scared, embarrassed, irritated, happy, disappointed, excited. Rate your
feelings: 0 per cent=no feeling; 100 per cent=strongest feeling.

Perfectionism area and situation	Perfectionism thoughts	Perfectionism behaviors	Feelings (rate 0–100 per cent)
Work, sending an email to a colleague	I have to be perfectly clear and succinct in how I write the email or I will seem incompetent (90 per cent)	Take 1 hour to check and keep rewording the email to make sure it is just right before sending	Anxious (75 per cent)

Reflection on Worksheet 7.1.2:
What did you learn about your perfectionism by completing this worksheet?

BOX 7.1.3 DEFINITIONS AND EXAMPLES OF SPECIFIC BEHAVIOR ASSOCIATED WITH PERFECTIONISM

Behavior	Definition	Examples
Avoidance	Attempting to decrease or escape from anxiety about a situation by not doing something	Not submitting assignments or work reports Not inviting friends to house for meals Not going out with friends to coffee Not training with other athletes
Procrastination	Attempting to decrease or escape from anxiety about a situation by delaying a task until a later time	Delaying writing assignment until the night before it is due Delaying cleaning house Delaying starting urgent work reports for the day, and surfing the internet instead
Performance checking	Checking how one is doing in a perfectionism area. It includes:	
	Testing – testing out performance repeatedly	Testing – checking body shape repeatedly for fat; re-reading work over and over; scrutinizing how well one said something after speaking

	Comparing – comparing oneself to how others are doing	*Comparing –* comparing number of hours worked to colleagues; comparing marks to other students; comparing own attractiveness to other people; comparing speed of running to other athletes
	Reassurance seeking – seeking reassurance from others about performance	*Reassurance seeking –* asking boss if report was OK several times; repeatedly apologizing for food at a dinner party; asking partner repeatedly if he/she thinks you are a good parent
Counter-productive behavior	Attempting to guard against or reduce the impact of something one feels anxious about in a way that 'backfires' and can make the situation worse	Always making lists before starting work Always sharpening pencils at the start and finish of a work day Always wearing make-up before leaving the house Ordering objects on desk before beginning study for the day Consuming exactly the same breakfast each day before starting athletic training

QUIZ (1)

You might want to complete the following quiz to help find out the areas in which behaviors associated with perfectionism are a problem for you. You can also use some of these questions as the basis for your survey (see Section 7.3) if they are relevant.

Answer the following questions using this scale:
1 = never, 2 = rarely, 3 = sometimes, 4 = very often, 5 = always

Home

1 How often do you spend more than five minutes making the bed?
2 How often do you spend more than 20 minutes cleaning the kitchen?
3 How often do you clean behind the fridge?
4 How often do you vacuum the bedrooms?
5 How often do you do clean the windows upstairs?
6 How often do you iron underwear?
7 How often do your standards interfere with the completion of household chores?
8 How often do you thoroughly clean the oven, including the racks?
9 How often do you check the cleanliness of your house over and over again?

Work

10 How often do you put off doing work because you're afraid of failing/not doing it right?
11 How often do you find it difficult starting tasks because you're afraid of failing or not doing it right?
12 How often do you check your work for mistakes?
13 How often do you procrastinate because you know that you're overly thorough and the task will take a long time?
14 How often do you find it difficult completing tasks because of your standards?
15 How often do you work overtime to complete a task to make sure it is right?
16 How often do your standards interfere with the completion of a task?

Social

17 How often do you ruminate about past social interactions?
18 How often do you arrange social meetings?
19 How often do you avoid social interactions?
20 How often do you check for reassurance from your friends?
21 How often do you put off social interactions by doing other tasks?
22 How often do you socialize with groups larger than two people?

QUIZ (2)

Hobbies
23 How often do you participate in your hobbies?
24 How often do you participate in group activities?
25 How often do you participate in individual hobbies?
26 How often do you check your achievement in a hobby?
27 How often do you avoid participating in a hobby?
28 How often do you ruminate about your performance in a hobby?
29 How often do your standards interfere with your achievement in a hobby?

Appearance
30 How often do you wash?
31 How often do you wash your hair?
32 How often do you do you brush your teeth?
33 How often do you go out without your make-up or hair done?
34 How often do you clean your ears?
35 How often do you cut/file your nails?
36 How often do you look in a mirror?
37 How often do you check your appearance?

Other questions
38 How important is the completion of a task to you?
39 What sort of checks do you make on a day-to-day basis?
40 What influence do the standards you set yourself have on the tasks that you undertake?
41 Are there any other specific perfectionist behaviors that you carry out?

Source: adapted from the Clinical Perfectionism Questionnaire developed by Fairburn and colleagues

Now you should have a good idea about the sorts of behaviors associated with perfectionism. In the next worksheet (7.1.3) you are asked to record your thoughts associated with perfectionism, the emotions that arise and then the behaviors that followed. These might include all those we have noted – avoidance, procrastination, performance checking, counter-productive behaviors – or only some of them. An example is provided for Rob, who has perfectionism in the area of work.

Rob: An example of perfectionism in the area of work

Rob is a 38-year-old married insurance broker, who is recognized by his colleagues as achieving excellent sales results and being very thorough in producing detailed monthly sales reports. Despite this, Rob worries about his performance, compares his work to that of colleagues in his team, and often feels disappointed in his performance. Rob now finds that he is delaying starting writing reports, putting it off for days on end, and will spend many hours worrying about what he is going to write and reading over his colleagues' reports; on occasion he has not handed reports to his boss by the due time because of his procrastination. He is working longer and longer hours every day, and working every weekend, but finds that he is falling behind with his reports, which is making him feel even more concerned about his work performance.

Now complete Worksheet 7.1.3. An example for Rob is provided for guidance.

Through monitoring your behaviors in Worksheet 7.1.3, did you become aware of the impact that your perfectionist thoughts have on a range of things you do? You will probably have found that much of your behavior during the day is influenced by perfectionism.

Now you have completed the monitoring suggested in this section, you are likely to have a much better understanding of how your perfectionism works. This includes the areas of your life affected by perfectionism and the particular behaviors and negative feelings that your perfectionism causes. This understanding will help you to use the techniques outlined in the following sections – the compartments of your toolkit – including testing out your perfectionist predictions and changing your unhelpful thinking.

WORKSHEET 7.1.3: MONITORING RECORD OF PERFECTIONISM THOUGHTS, EMOTIONS AND BEHAVIORS

Thought	Emotion	Avoidance	Procrastination	Performance checking	Counterproductive behaviors
I need to write a really good report – it's so important	Fear, anxiety	Not submitting report and asking boss for extension of deadline until following week	Putting off writing the report due at the end of the week, each day worrying but delaying starting	*Testing* – reading comments on previous reports over and over *Comparing* – Reading my colleagues' reports over and over *Reassurance seeking* – Asking my partner repeatedly whether she thinks I can do the report well	Lining up business cards over and over Writing detailed lists daily of tasks to be done towards the report

Reflection on Worksheet 7.1.3:
What did you learn about your perfectionism by completing this worksheet?

TAKE-HOME MESSAGE

- Self-monitoring is important as it helps you to understand your perfectionism and become more objective about it.
- Self-monitoring can include identifying areas of perfectionism and monitoring perfectionism thoughts, emotions and behavior (avoidance, procrastination, performance checking, counterproductive behaviors).

7.2 Psychoeducation

We all hold beliefs about the 'right' way that tasks should be completed and the 'right' way to behave. For example, you may think that the 'right' way to read this book is chapter by chapter, thoroughly and without skipping anything. You may have a point – but the occasional foray into chapters a bit ahead that look interesting won't do a great deal of harm. Our beliefs about 'right' and 'wrong' concern both simple everyday tasks – such as making the bed, making breakfast, tidying up and showering – and more complex activities, such as having a successful relationship. Behind such beliefs are often other beliefs concerning the 'facts' of the situation. For example, you might believe it to be a 'fact' that if you shower for five minutes then you are just as clean as if you shower for 20 minutes. You might believe that if you leave the breakfast dishes out for a couple of hours then the food will attract flies and ants. Having read articles in the newspapers by relationship experts, you may hold the view that the most successful relationships are those where the couple split the household chores 50:50. When you're thinking about making changes to your personal standards and behavior, it's important to know how much of your beliefs is fact and how much is hearsay or myth – fiction.

Fact vs fiction

Later in this chapter we discuss tackling personal beliefs by testing them out using surveys (Section 7.3) and behavioral experiments (Section 7.4). It's important to get hold of the right factual information as the foundation for this later work – as illustrated by the example of Bernie.

Bernie: The 80:20 principle is a proven fact

Bernie was a 52-year-old management consultant who, ten years earlier, had come across the 80:20 principle in a management course. The 80:20 principle is also known as 'Pareto's Law'. In the management course, the 80:20 principle was defined as the principle that 80 per cent of the results flow from just 20 per cent of the causes. Examples were given: that 20 per cent of products account for 80 per cent of sales, 20 per cent of motorists cause 80 per cent of accidents and 20 per cent of your clothes are worn 80 per cent of the time. Much of the course concentrated on a book on this principle (by Richard Koch), which describes how you can achieve much more by concentrating on the 20 per cent of the causes. Using this principle was described as 'the key to controlling our lives'. What Bernie took home from the course was that if she went the extra mile – put in an extra 20 per cent of effort above what most people did – then she would achieve more than ever and be more in control of her life than before. She had misunderstood the principle, and she was also extending the principle to situations where its application had not been researched – her own personal situations. She decided that where she would normally stop her preparation for work, she would go on for another 20 per cent of the original time. Where she would normally just quickly make the bed, she spent extra time making sure it was done properly and 'going the extra mile'. She felt the principle was working: she perceived the extra effort to be paying off in terms of results, and for a long time she felt it was worth the extra time. Over the next few months she became increasingly exhausted and isolated, but was reluctant to give up the perceived benefits of putting in that extra 20 per cent.

Bernie's belief that she was achieving more because she was putting in 100 per cent of effort compared to most people's 80 per cent was driving a great deal of her behavior. In treatment, she and her therapist began by trying to understand what was keeping her difficulties going, following the process we outlined in Chapter 5. Her belief about the 80:20 rule was clearly part of the problem. The therapist had to confess to knowing nothing about the principle, but both agreed to go and research the information and find out the facts. It quickly emerged that Bernie both had misunderstood the principle and was applying it to situations for which it had not been intended. Did this change Bernie's perfectionism? No, not overnight. However, finding out the correct information was a very important part of the process of changing and led her to test some of her other beliefs using methods such as surveys, diaries and behavioral experiments.

The harder you work, the better you'll do: Fact or fiction?

It is necessary to test this personal belief with an experiment, as described in Section 7.4, but information about the general principle of the relationship between hard work and success is important as well. How many of us have been told that we could achieve more if we worked harder? How many teachers have written a report saying that grades could be improved with just a little more effort? Is this true? Intuitively it seems that if someone puts in no work (doesn't revise for an exam, for example) then they will do less well than someone who puts in a great deal of work. However, it does not follow that the harder you work (or the more you practice or train), the better you will do. Achievement, it turns out, is actually the result of a great many factors that are all interrelated. Yes, it is necessary to put in *some* effort; but factors such as personal interest, ability, class sizes, peer support and mental health all influence actual achievement. Putting in some effort is necessary for achievement but it is not sufficient. Putting in too much may backfire due to the impact of exhaustion. It is also unhelpful because it perpetuates the belief held by some people that they are only achieving because they tried so hard and that they are naturally less able than others.

This fact is well known among athletes, where it underlies what is known as 'over-training'. Athletes who have perfectionism will often 'over-train', that is, add extra training sessions on top of what their coach recommends. This might involve secretly slipping in extra training sessions away from the training group, and not reporting these to their coach. They have to do this secretly because they know that if others find out they will say they are training 'too much'; but they believe that they must train harder than the others, and that they will only do well if they train harder and put in more sessions than the other athletes. The problem with this is that there is only a certain amount of training athletes can do before they become exhausted and their body becomes injured. Thus over-training often leads to injuries in athletes (e.g. stress fractures in the legs from too much running) which can put them out of training altogether for months on end. So instead of the extra training having the desired effect of helping them to win a race, it can end up by forcing the athlete to stop training completely and do nothing but walk for six months. Which route, then, actually leads to better performance for the athlete? The perfectionist drive to do ever more work and over-train, or a more balanced approach to training involving adequate rest days and following the coach's advice?

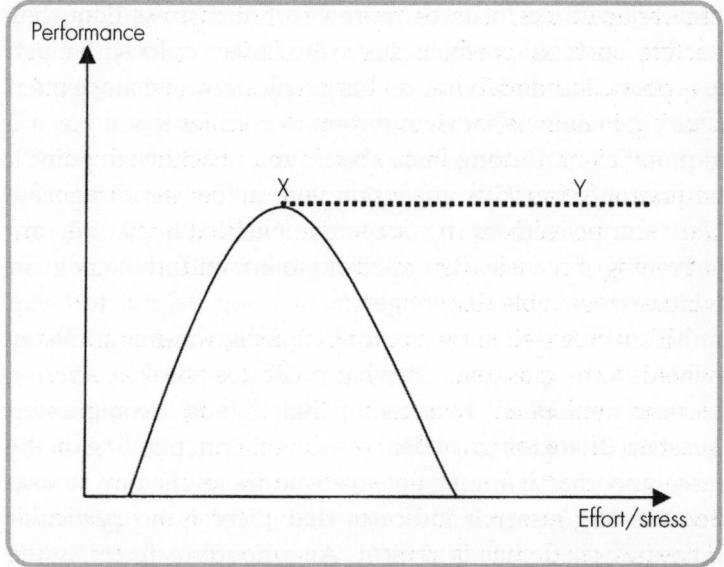

Figure 7.2.1 The connection between stress and performance

Facts about perfectionism and performance

There is a big research literature on how perfectionism affects performance, particularly in the field of sport and exercise. One influential approach is known as the 'Yerkes–Dodson Law' stemming back to 1908. Yerkes and Dodson noticed that there was an inverted U-shaped relationship between effort/stress and performance. Performance was best when there wasn't too much or too little stress. Other research has supported the idea that too much stress/arousal can negatively affect performance. The relationship is shown in Figure 7.2.1 above.

In our experience, it isn't that people with perfectionism are typically putting in so much effort that their performance is extremely bad. Rather, it strikes us that, in many cases, they are putting in much more effort and stress than they need to, and could in fact achieve the same results with much less effort. The dotted line on the graph shows what we often see in the clinic. What is important to know is that if you are at point Y on the dotted line above, you can move to point X without any negative impact on your actual performance – just an improvement in your stress levels. Whether you are at point X or Y is clearly important to know, and the point at which stress/arousal changes from being helpful to being unhelpful for you is the six million dollar question, closely related to the question, 'At what point does healthy striving become unhelpful?' It turns out that this is a complicated question (there is a great deal of variability depending on the task) and that it might not even be the right one to ask, because the research indicates that there is no particular universal *point* that is critical. An important factor is the person's reaction to perceived failure. Negative reactions to mistakes and perceived imperfections (which invariably happens to people who have the type of perfectionism we're discussing) can have a detrimental effect on achievement. The example of Soo-Lee illustrates how this can happen.

Soo-Lee: A triathlete

Soo-Lee was a 25-year-old triathlete who always enjoyed pushing her body and her mind as far as they would go. She was a very sociable person and although not the best triathlete in her club, she was in the top three and that was good enough for her. She would not have considered herself to be a perfectionist. Her friends, however, did think that she was a perfectionist. She would dwell on every conversation that she had, looking to see what she had said wrong and whether she had accidentally offended someone. If someone did not call her back, she would rack her brain trying to think of what she had said to them that could cause them not to like her. She would usually focus on something she had said, or the way she had said it, and would be highly critical of herself. This tendency to find a mistake and then be very self-critical was beginning to impact on her relationships as she was constantly either seeking reassurance from her friends or canceling arrangements because she couldn't stand the invariable self-examination that would result. She was also beginning to experience problems training with her club – she found she was re-playing her races repeatedly in her head and telling herself off for having lost time, for example by doing slow transitions, and over-thinking about all the places where she should have pushed herself harder. Her enjoyment of the sport was beginning to decrease because she was getting less positive feelings from exercising now that she was beginning to think during races about how she should be going faster and improving her technique, and whether she would get home and worry about it all night. She became less and less motivated to train, and did not do so well in her races; this increased her frustration and made her think that triathlons were not for her. She gradually lost contact with her club and her friends, since seeing them was a reminder for her that she was a failure with no friends and no outside interests.

For Soo-Lee, the facts of the situation were that focusing on her mistakes and being self-critical were having a negative impact on her performance. It wouldn't have mattered if she had trained more; it was what was going on inside her head that was affecting both her enjoyment and her achievement. Focusing on mistakes can lead to a variety of emotional reactions – sadness, disappointment, frustration and fury are common – and it is these that interfere with performance.

This information is important, because the treatment in this book is not about having to accept that you will do things less well or achieve less. In fact, it is as much about you achieving more, because hopefully you will be changing some of the beliefs and behaviors that are stopping you from achieving. It is also important to know, though, that by the end of the book your self-esteem will probably be less based on striving and achievement than at present so that you can have more choice and more control over your life.

Facts about efficiency

Joachim Stoeber and his colleagues have been interested in perfectionism for many years and have raised the important notion of *efficiency*. This is about not just absolute performance, but the right amount of effort to achieve the desired level of performance. Too much effort might be wasted and indeed backfire by causing exhaustion, low mood, and the other negative effects we have mentioned. Too little effort will be insufficient to attain the desired outcome. The formula for the rest of your life to guide you about the right amount of effort to put into each task is given in the box below.

Formula for right amount of effort to obtain optimal outcome:

If the box above is blank in your copy of this book, it is not a mistake. *There is no magic formula.* If there were, the process of writing this book might have been very different – and so would much of all of our lives. We have to work this out for ourselves by trial and error, and much of the time it can seem like mostly error! Any 'fact' or 'formula' would only ever be a general principle – what is important is how it works for you. By making a note of the effort you are putting in and the outcomes you are getting, and reflecting on the importance of each task, you will begin to find a formula (or more likely, many formulas) that work for you in a variety of situations.

What are the facts about efficiency? In a Japanese study on solving problems, researchers found that people who had lots of perfectionist thoughts and beliefs did worse on the task than those who scored low in perfectionism. They concluded that those who were highly perfectionist were spending more time looking at irrelevant information in an attempt to be thorough than those who were less perfectionist, and that this impaired their performance. In another study looking at perfectionism and efficiency in proofreading, again there was support for the notion that high levels of perfectionism were associated with reduced efficiency. Again, perfectionism was also associated with worse performance in the task, in this case because those with high levels of perfectionism incorrectly identified more errors on the proofreading task than those with low levels of perfectionism.

Facts about risk

In our work with people with obsessive compulsive disorder who have a fear of contamination, it is important to find out the facts about germs and diseases. For example, a patient with perfectionism and OCD was very worried about catching HIV from a cash machine. We worked together to find out the actual facts about this – how many people have HIV, how long does the virus live, have there ever been any documented cases of people catching HIV this way? Similarly, when we have had patients with a fear of choking it has been an important part of treatment to find out how many people die from choking each year and how many die as the result of other incidents, to enable the patient to understand fully and then accept the level of risk involved. The kind of information that you will need to overcome your perfectionism is likely to be very particular to you, and it is important to know where to go to get *reliable* information. Some websites, for instance, 'scaremonger' and others just express personal points of view. Other websites are extremely thorough and medically oriented but difficult to find your way around. Use reputable websites from universities or respected national organizations. You will find some suggestions in the sections on 'useful' and 'essential' websites at the end of this book.

Fact and fiction: What we tell our patients

What we tell our patients varies according to their specific concerns, but we do usually impart some factual information before we go on to the gathering of personal information through surveys, diaries and experiments. We therefore set out here the ten statements that most commonly come up when we are helping patients to sort out fact from fiction.

1 *'The harder someone works, the better they do.'* This is not the case, as illustrated above; remember the example of the athlete who over-trains and ends up injured.
2 *'Successful people work harder than less successful people.'* This is not the case either; you may find this easier to accept if you think of some people you know, or know of, who are successful and yet have a balanced life.

3 *'To get ahead you have to be single-minded and give up all outside interests.'* Again, thinking of those who are successful (e.g. Richard Branson) quickly calls this belief into question.

4 *'Clever people don't have to work so hard as stupid people.'* Wrong again. There is no relationship between cleverness and hard work.

5 *'I feel a fraud.'* Lots of people feel a fraud (see Section 7.3 on 'surveys'). That doesn't mean they are.

6 *'The more you put into something, the more you get out of it.'* This is sometimes true for some people, but not always true for all people or indeed every activity.

7 *'People notice every little detail and are quick to form critical judgments.'* People notice less than you think. In studies from Daniel Simons's laboratory on 'change blindness', a large proportion of people don't notice if an entire person changes.* It is very unlikely that your friends will notice a bit of mess in your house.

8 *'People can't be happy if they're not successful.'* This is simply not true. What is more, the construct of 'success' itself isn't black and white but is complicated.

9 *'If I avoid a problem, then it tends to sort itself out.'* Although we all wish this were true, and it may be a useful strategy in some situations, sustained avoidance of important matters is rarely a good strategy.

10 *'If a job's worth doing, it's worth doing well.'* This may be a good general principle, but it doesn't apply to everything. For example, sometimes it is worth ironing badly so that your partner doesn't ask you to do the ironing again!

---

* http://viscog.beckman.illinois.edu/djs_lab/overviewCB.html

TAKE-HOME MESSAGE

- Know your facts.
- Know your facts.
- Know your facts.

This is not an error – the key message is to know your facts.

7.3 Surveys

In the previous section we discussed the importance of finding out the facts about perfectionism. This is an essential part of knowing what is reasonable and what is not, and what is 'normal'. However, sometimes the information that is required is not in the public domain, and it is necessary to get some personalized information. It is very common for people with perfectionism to fear what other people might think or how they might react, and this can feed the fear of failure and concern over mistakes and criticism that is at the heart of perfectionism. It is therefore important to find out the reality about what other people think and do, and how they respond to various situations, so that beliefs about other people's beliefs and reactions can be tested. This sort of very particular, personal information can be obtained using a method called 'surveying'.

'Surveys' to overcome perfectionism are much like any other survey. They are designed to gather information about what people think and how they behave. To contribute to overcoming perfectionism, they have to be highly personalized. In fact, no two surveys are ever quite the same. Surveys can be used to find out what people might do or think in particular situations, but they can also be used to gain information about the extent of particular perfectionist behaviors in people who do not find perfectionism a problem. Such information can help 'set the bar' for striving and achievement at a realistic level. Take the case of Hannah shown here.

Hannah: Beliefs about being tidy

Hannah was a 43-year-old mother of four. People joked that she was 'obsessional' about her house and indeed she was very houseproud. She had raised her children not to make a mess, to take toys out only one at a time and to put their toys away immediately after use. As well as ironing all the children's clothes and her own clothes, she ironed bedsheets, underwear, towels and sports clothes. Needless to say, this ironing took up a great deal of her time, but she enjoyed seeing her children look neatly presented. She believed that there was 'a place for everything and everything in its place'. She had functioned well like this for many years, but she was too tired in the evening to give her partner much time or attention. Their relationship was under stress and she had no interest in intimacy. She was unable to entertain friends in the house or allow her children to have friends over because of the amount of work it would entail for her tidying up afterwards. Her sister complained that she could not relax when she came to visit out of fear of putting something away in the wrong place. Hannah recognized that her need for orderliness and tidiness in the home was excessive, but she believed that it was only slightly more than other people's. She also believed that most people thought that she was in control of her life because of her tidy home and the appearance of her children, and she valued this.

In treatment, the therapist suggested that perhaps most people do not actually iron their underwear or bedsheets, and that actually many people would think she was out of control of her life because of her excessive need for tidiness. It was agreed that together the therapist and Hannah would construct a survey to find out (a) what other people did about ironing and (b) what they thought of people (not specifically Hannah) who had a tidy home and appearance.

The results of the survey of eight of Hannah's friends was surprising to both the therapist and Hannah. Six out of the eight did actually iron their underwear and two ironed bedsheets; two said that an extremely tidy home and appearance led them to think that the person 'had nothing better to do' or should 'get a life'; four said that they did not think anything in particular about whether someone was in control of their life or not because they had a tidy home and appearance; and two said that they thought a tidy person and appearance meant the person was organized.

Hannah and her therapist discussed the results and the range of reactions. It was common among Hannah's friends to iron underwear but not bedsheets, and this was interesting information for Hannah about what was reasonable and what was perhaps not. The range of reactions to someone who was excessively tidy prompted Hannah to re-evaluate some of her motivation for tidiness and led directly to a discussion about Hannah's need for tidiness and control, irrespective of what other people think.

Troubleshooting

Surveys can be difficult to do if you are isolated and have few social contacts. In face-to-face therapy, the therapist will often do the survey among his/her own friends and colleagues in such situations. If you do not have a therapist, and have few friends, then perhaps turning to the internet and people on social networking sites such as Facebook or Twitter might help with the survey.

The other problem with surveys is that constructing them can be difficult. You can do many separate surveys, so it can be helpful to narrow each one down by thinking what type of information you need to help set your standards at a more reasonable level, or what beliefs you want to test so that you can tackle your fear of failure.

Surveys to help set standards

Think back to Section 7.1, in which we asked you to identify the area(s) in which you had problems with perfectionism. Your survey will vary according to the sort of area in which you are having difficulties. Often your questions will be about how frequently someone engages in a behavior or how long they spend doing something. Some examples are given in Box 7.3.1.

You can also use the quiz from Section 7.1 to help construct your survey.

Constructing your own survey to test beliefs

The type of perfectionism we have been discussing in this book is self-motivated. People with this type of perfectionism are driving themselves to achieve not because they are concerned about what other people think, but because their self-evaluation is overly dependent on striving and achievement. Despite this important distinction, there are often times when what other people think is very closely related to self-evaluation and perfectionism, and it may therefore be useful to examine such beliefs. In Hannah's case, she was tidying the house because she believed it was the right thing to do, because it gave her a sense of control *and* because she believed that other people would think she was out of control if her house was a mess.

Surveys will typically contain more than one question, but not too many: the ideal survey contains between three and eight questions, which won't be too onerous for the person completing it. Sometimes it is necessary to test several beliefs, for example about successful people, within a single survey, because it is not always easy to find people to complete the survey; this is fine, again provided that the

BOX 7.3.1 SOME EXAMPLES OF SURVEY QUESTIONS

Area	Q1	Q2	Q3	Q4
Tidiness	How long do you spend tidying each day?	How often do you vacuum?	How often do you dust?	How long does it take you to make the bed?
Avoidance/ procrastination	How often do you avoid doing tasks that you know will be time-consuming?	How often you avoid so much that you miss the deadline?	How much trouble do you get in because of your avoidance/procrastination?	Are there some things you avoid more than others? What are they?
Work	How long do you spend preparing a document?	How many times do you go over and over the document?	Do you often stay up all night to get the words in a presentation/document 'just right'?	Do you ever make yourself ill because you work so hard?
Social	How often do you replay conversations over and over in your head?	If you replay them, do you always focus on just the negative or do you go over the whole thing?	How much do you try to say 'just the right thing' in social situations?	How much preparation do you do for a social event, e.g. searching on the internet for information about the hostess?
Music	How often do you practise and for how long?	Do you ever practise really quickly/not properly?	Do you practise even when you are injured?	Do you practise even when there is an alternative social event?
Gardening	How long do you garden for at any one time?	How do you make sure you pull up all the weeds?	After pulling up the weeds, how often do you check they haven't grown back?	Do you garden in the dark?
Emails	How long does it take you to write an email?	How often do you check through your email?	Do you spellcheck your email before sending it?	Do you keep every email you have ever sent or received?

survey isn't too long. Some examples of beliefs that can be usefully tested with surveys are given in Box 7.3.2, with suggestions about questions and whom you might ask to complete the survey.

BOX 7.3.2 WHAT BELIEFS CAN BE TESTED BY SURVEYS, WHOM TO ASK AND WHAT TO ASK THEM: SOME EXAMPLES

Belief	Survey questions
I make more mistakes than other people.	*This survey would be given primarily to people that the person respected.* In the last month, how many 'mistakes' have you made (e.g. forgotten an appointment, sent an email with a spelling error in it, said something you later regretted)?
The mistakes I make are worse than other people's mistakes.	*This survey would be given primarily to people that the person respected.* Please list as many of the 'mistakes' you have made in the last month as possible. 'Mistakes' would include giving the wrong change, forgetting to do something, snapping at someone. Please rate how bad you think the mistake was on a scale of 0 (not at all) to 10 (extremely). What consequences did your mistake have? Do you think other people make similar mistakes?

Doing well at work comes naturally to other people but I have to work at it.	*This survey would be given to people that are objectively successful at work.* How much are you achieving in your work/studies? Please rate from 0 (not at all) to 10 (extremely) How much would you say your success 'came naturally'? Please rate from 0 (not at all) to 10 (extremely) How much would you say you had to work at your success? Please rate from 0 (not at all) to 10 (extremely) What are the reasons for your success?
I am a 'fraud' and will be discovered.	*The aim of this survey is to demonstrate that the belief that one is a 'fraud' and will be discovered is extremely common. It would be given to someone whose opinion the person respected.* How much do you believe you are a 'fraud' and will be discovered? Please rate from 0 (not at all) to 10 (extremely) What are the reasons for your success?
Successful people always take their BlackBerrys away with them.	*This survey would be given to people who are objectively successful at work.* Do you check email when you are on holiday?

	Do you take work calls when you are on holiday? Do you believe that having a complete break from work helps you 'recharge your batteries' and therefore be more successful when you return?
People don't respect 'slackers'.	What do you think of people who work excessively hard? What do you think of people who work moderately hard? What do you think of people who do the minimum of the work necessary to get the job done? What do you think of people who let other people do their work for them?
Being early for a meeting or social event is simply 'wasting time'.	What do you think of people who arrive extremely early for a meeting/social event? What do you think of people who arrive approximately 10 minutes before a meeting/social event? What do you think of people who arrive just in time for a meeting/social event? What do you think of people who arrive a few minutes after the start of a meeting/social event? What do you think of people who arrive late for a social event?

Successful people don't watch trashy TV or read trashy magazines.	*This survey would be given to people who are objectively successful.* Do you watch soap operas? Do you read 'trashy' magazines such as *OK* or *Hello*? Do you know any successful people who do watch 'trashy' TV or read 'trashy magazines'? Would you be less successful if you did read/watch 'trash'?
If I went out without make-up, people would think I was a slob.	*You would want to record whether the responses were given by men or women.* What do you think of women who go out during the day without any make-up? What do you think of women who go out at night to a party without any make-up? What do you think of women who always wear make-up to everything? What do you think of women who wear too much make-up?
Most people believe that 'if a job is worth doing, it is worth doing well'.	Do you believe that 'if a job is worth doing, it is worth doing well'? Are there any exceptions to this? Can you give an example of when you have not done a job as thoroughly as it could have been done because you had other priorities?

Most people wouldn't choose the 'easy way out'.	If you could achieve the same goal by really pushing yourself, working hard and focusing day and night or by taking an 'easier' option, which would you choose? Do you believe there is any value in pushing yourself to achieve a particular goal if there were an alternative, easier way? Can you give some examples?
Successful people are not overweight.	Do you believe that successful people are not overweight? Do you know anyone who is successful and overweight? Please state who. Do you know anyone who is successful and average weight? Please state who. Do you know anyone who is successful and underweight? Please state who.
My children are naughtier than other people's children.	*This would only be given to the primary caregiver of children of a similar age to yours. Ask people to answer the asterisked questions on a scale from 0 (not at all) to 10 (extremely).* *How naughty are your children? How many times to you have to tell them to do something before they do it? *How often do your children 'talk back' to you?*

	*How often do your children call you names? *How often do your children get out of bed at night? *How often do you end up shouting at your children? *How often do your children take food without asking?
Other people don't want to hear about my problems so I should always present a 'perfect' front.	What do you think about people who never share their problems? What do you think about people who always present a front of 'everything is rosy'? Who would you choose to spend time with – someone who discussed their personal issues or someone for whom 'everything is rosy'? Why?
Christmas cards should have a personalized message.	Do you write a personalized message in Christmas cards? If so, why? If not, why not? Do you know if someone has written you a personalized message? What do you think of people who write a short, general message in Christmas cards? What do you think of people who send a general, typed A4 circular letter with all their news in their Christmas cards? Do you think Christmas cards should have a personalized message?

What to do with the information from surveys

Collect the responses

Having constructed your survey and given it out, you need to collect the responses. Depending on how you drew it up, you will have some information about where other people set the standard (e.g. what is the average length of time they take to make the bed in the morning) or some information to test a belief (e.g. that successful people are thin). If you can, do a summary table or graph to make the information that you've collected as clear as possible.

Reflect on the responses

The responses to the survey are likely to contain some surprises. It may be that most people never clean behind the fridge, or that most people clean behind the fridge weekly. What usually happens, though, is that there is a *range* of responses. There will be some people cleaning weekly, and others who never clean. There are likely to be some people who think that sending a general typed A4 circular letter with Christmas cards is an excellent idea because it means you get to hear what is going on, and others who think that it is terrible. Some people will think badly of a woman who always goes out with make-up on, whereas others might think badly of a woman who never wears make-up.

Hopefully there will be at least three outcomes from the survey, as follows.

REALITY CHECK

The survey is a 'reality' check about your standards and beliefs. You now know more about what is 'normal' and about what other people think. Equipped with this information about reality, you can now choose to think about adjusting your standards or possibly re-examining your beliefs. What you might have to accept is that you do not make *more* mistakes than other people, or *worse* mistakes than other people, but that successful people usually do actually take their BlackBerrys away with them. The information should help you focus on what the reality is that you need to accept, and what is not a reality but more of a personal belief that can continue to be examined and changed.

IDENTIFYING ALL OR NOTHING THINKING

What often emerges from a survey is that there is no consensus, no 'right and wrong', and that the answers are not 'black and white'. Usually, some people think one way and others think another. Some believe that a particular behavior is necessary for success, and others do not. The range of responses should help with the notion that beliefs, behavior and simply living are rather complicated and that there is a middle ground that can be taken. This conclusion will lead naturally to testing your beliefs using the strategies in Section 7.5.

PROVIDING A BASIS FOR BEHAVIORAL EXPERIMENTS

The information from the survey will hopefully lead naturally to further examining of some of your beliefs about striving and achievement. For example, the results of the survey may have indicated that people prefer to spend time with people who disclose some personal issues rather than those who present a 'perfect' front. You may still doubt whether this is really true or whether it is just a response in a survey. The key to changing beliefs is to gather as much evidence as possible about the reality using a variety of methods so that old beliefs that are no longer sustainable can be replaced by new, more realistic beliefs. At this point you have some information about what people think about people who present a 'perfect' front, but further information is likely to be required. Conducting a behavioral experiment of the type described in the next section will help you to gather more information to enable you to re-examine this belief.

TAKE-HOME MESSAGE

- Surveys can be used to gather information about 'normal' standards and about beliefs.
- The results of the survey will be a 'reality check'.
- The information from the survey should begin the process of helping to adjust your standards and beliefs, but further work on 'all or nothing thinking' or conducting behavioral experiments will be needed.

7.4 Behavioral experiments

Questioning your behavior

By now you will have begun to gather some information that calls into question some of the thoughts and assumptions you previously held about the 'right' way to do things. You will have learned that some of your previously held beliefs might not be true, and the surveys will have given you more valuable information about the way the world works in reality and what other people may think. The next step is to question whether some of the things you do to help you are working the way you think they are or whether they are actually backfiring and causing more problems than they solve.

The principles of behavioral experiments

The goal of a behavioral experiment is to gather information to help test a belief about some action or behavior. For example, if you believed that writing something down about an accident will cause it to happen, you would test that belief by writing it down. You probably think that doing so would cause great anxiety and that the anxiety would continue for hours. Such beliefs can also be tested within the same experiment by making a note of the extent of the anxiety and its duration. If you believe that your work will receive a worse mark if you spend three hours on it rather than six hours, that belief can be tested by giving in a piece of work on which you have spent three and then another (as similar as possible) piece of work on which you have spent six hours. Similarly, if you're a teacher who is used to writing completely individual reports for each child, which is very time-consuming, you might want to write more standardized reports to save time. Such an experiment could test your belief that if the reports were standardized you would attract comment from the head teacher and criticism from parents, that you would worry, and so on. Behavioral experiments are a very good way of testing your predictions and gathering personalized, meaningful information. They're hard to do – it takes courage to put yourself on the spot in this way – but if you don't test how far your beliefs and behaviors match up to reality, it's unlikely that you'll change.

Behavioral experiment to address checking

Jeff the plumber

Jeff was an attractive, friendly and sociable 29-year-old plumber in a long-term relationship with his girlfriend. He worked for a small plumbing company and was the most senior of the three plumbers employed. He had been with the company since the start and was very motivated to make the enterprise a success. Jeff worked extremely hard, and covered the shifts that the other two plumbers did not want to do (Saturday nights, evenings and weekends). He felt it was his responsibility to do this as he was the most senior of the three. Jeff also dealt with the financial side of his plumbing work – giving customers bills and processing their payments, giving change, etc. When he came for therapy he was extremely agitated, having feared that he might have given a customer the wrong change. He had contacted the customer, who had told him not to worry (the sum was minimal) but Jeff could not get out of his mind that he had made such a mistake over something as important as giving change to his customer. He replayed the scene where he had handed over the change again and again, trying to focus in on the coins to be certain whether he had given the wrong amount. He replayed the conversation with the customer again and again in his mind, trying to detect whether the customer was genuine when he said 'not to worry' or if the customer's tone implied that he thought that Jeff was a criminal and had taken the money on purpose. This incident had taken place three months earlier, and Jeff was now repeatedly checking all aspects of his plumbing work, in particular that taps were closed, several times. He had begun to phone clients to check that everything was OK, both with the plumbing and on the finance side, on the pretext of 'customer service'. He would then replay those conversations, trying to detect if the person was being polite when something really was wrong or if they were being genuine. His greatest difficulty, however, was with processing the invoices once each job was complete. Jeff was checking his calculations, the invoices and the financial processes to such an extent that it was taking an extra 30 minutes of the customer's time at the end of each job, and the customers were clearly getting frustrated. He feared he was jeopardizing the business and that it would close because of his checking behavior.

Jeff was checking both in his actions (repeatedly checking taps, repeatedly checking his calculations) and in his head (replaying the scene), and both aspects of checking are common in people with perfectionism. For people with social anxiety, repeatedly going over a social event is known as 'post-event processing', and it can cause a great deal of agitation. For Jeff, his checking was having real consequences for his customers, but he was 'catastrophizing' these consequences, imagining the worst-case scenario of the entire business being in jeopardy. It should also be noted that Jeff was working extremely hard – evenings and weekends – and having very little time off. When you're very tired it is harder to dismiss concerns and worries, and thoughts seem to 'take hold'.

Why was Jeff checking? The answer seems obvious – to make sure he wasn't making a mistake. However, evidence from recent research suggests that, contrary to what one might expect, repeated checking of this nature doesn't actually prevent more mistakes being made, and it doesn't actually improve memory. In fact, the real consequence of such repeated checking is that it *decreases confidence* in memory. In other words, the more you check, the more uncertain you become. This information was discussed with Jeff in therapy but it didn't take root because it didn't have personal relevance for him. We therefore conducted a behavioral experiment to test Jeff's belief that repeatedly checking helped him remember.

BOX 7.4.1 JEFF'S BEHAVIORAL EXPERIMENT TO TEST THE BELIEF THAT REPEATED CHECKING HELPS MEMORY AND HELPS REDUCE ANXIETY AND WORRY

Prediction

If I repeatedly check my calculations, I won't worry so much afterwards and will feel more certain I haven't short-changed someone than if I only check my calculations once.

Experiment

Day 1: Repeatedly check calculations as usual (or even more)

Make note of worry level (0–10) immediately after checking (0 = no worry, 10 = extreme worry) and again 1 hour later

Make note of certainty that haven't short-changed someone immediately after checking (0 = not certain; 10 = certain) and again 1 hour later

Day 2: Check calculations once and make same notes as above

Day 3: Repeatedly check calculations as usual (or even more) and make same notes as above

Day 4: Check calculations once and make same notes as above

Day 5: Repeatedly check calculations as usual (or even more) and make same notes as above

Day 6: Check calculations once and make same notes as above

Day 7: Review information gathered over previous six days

Results

	Worry immediately	Worry after 1 hr	Certainty immediately	Certainty after 1 hr
Checking repeatedly				
Day 1	8	7	1	2
Day 3	9	8	2	1
Day 5	8	7	1	1
Checking once				
Day 2	4	4	9	8
Day 4	4	2	9	9
Day 6	4	1	8	9

Interpreting the results

On the days that Jeff checked repeatedly, his worry immediately after checking was high (8 and 9). One hour later, the worry had come down a little but was still high (7 and 8). On these days, he was really uncertain (1 and 2) whether he had short-changed someone and after an hour he was still uncertain. It was at these times he had a strong urge to phone the customer to check that everything was OK. On the days that he checked once, contrary to his predictions, his worry was much lower (4) and lower still an hour later on days 4 and 6. Another real surprise was that he was much more certain (8 and 9) that he had not short-changed anyone on the days when he checked his calculations once, and his certainty remained strong one hour later. He had no urges on these days to call the customer, and he therefore didn't have additional conversations to 'check' in his head.

Other checking experiments

Jeff did many other checking experiments. He tested his belief that checking conversations in his head made him feel better than not checking, and that phoning clients left him feeling more certain that he hadn't made a mistake. What he found by doing all of these experiments was that his checking in fact made him feel more uncertain and anxious, and this meant he was able to stop this counterproductive behavior.

Behavioral experiment to address avoidance

Callie, the frustrated author

Callie was a 38-year-old working in human resources in a university. She had not intended to work in human resources; she had wanted to be an author after graduating with a first-class degree in English. She had actually written a book and it was almost complete. She had shown drafts of it to friends and family, who had all praised it, and she had contacted a publishing agent who told her to send a draft when it was finished. It had been about five years since the publishing agent had said this, and although Callie had done a little more work on the book since then, she hadn't been able to complete it. In fact, for the past three years she hadn't looked at it, although she thought about the ending and how it should be every day. Her family felt this was a terrible waste of her potential and she agreed. She was unable to articulate why she couldn't complete the book. Some aspect of her avoidance was a fear that it would be rejected by publishers, although she acknowledged that this happened all the time. Another aspect was that she couldn't find an ending that 'felt right'; all the endings she ran over in her head (and some attempts on paper) felt inadequate. She felt that she was a failure and pathetic for being unable to complete the book and send it off to the agent.

Callie had three predictions that she could test with behavioral experiments. The first was that her book would be rejected. The second was that no ending would 'feel right'. The third, related to this, was that the feeling of it 'not being right' would prey on her mind for a long time, causing distress.

A series of behavioral experiments were conducted with Callie to help her build up to being able to complete her book and test the prediction that it would be rejected. The first set of experiments were about 'not feeling right'. This feeling wasn't just restricted to the book but occurred in a variety of situations. She often felt that the reports she needed to submit at work 'weren't right', and so she avoided doing them until the very last minute. For her first experiment, she completed two reports. One was completed at the very last minute despite her feeling that it 'wasn't right'. The other was completed ahead of time. She had predicted that if she submitted the report earlier, then her discomfort associated with it 'not being right' would last longer than if she did it at the last minute and therefore would cause her more distress. In actual fact, when she submitted the report ahead of time, she felt a sense of achievement about it not being rushed and she didn't perceive it to be either more or less right than the report she submitted right on the deadline. She learned from this that submitting a report ahead of time didn't increase her feelings of 'not rightness' but did give her a sense of achievement. It also reduced her worry because she found that the report wasn't 'hanging over her head'.

Callie did more behavioral experiments to find out what influenced the feelings of being 'not right' – for example, whether it was tiredness, mood or circumstances – and to see how long the feeling lasted (she predicted it would remain constant all day, every day). This behavioral experiment was very simple: she simply monitored her feeling of 'not rightness' and found that it waxed and waned throughout the day depending on what she was doing. After doing more than six experiments, she agreed to write a single ending for the book despite acknowledging that it wouldn't be 'right'.

Callie then sent her book off to the publishing agent – who rejected it with little explanation. Callie was remarkably resilient, saying that she felt she now had the capacity to work on the book some more and complete it properly so she could send it to other publishers. Although she had known rationally that avoidance wasn't helping, it was her personal experience of conducting very small, specific behavioral experiments that helped her overcome it.

Different forms of behavioral experiments

Behavioral experiments can take a variety of different forms. Some are straightforward – monitoring how anxious you will be in a particular situation, what will happen if you do something, how long an emotion might last, how other people might react. Sometimes they are more complicated and involve contrasting one behavior with another; for example, in Jeff's case he contrasted repeated checking with a single check. The key point about all of them is that behavioral experiments test predictions and provide personally relevant, meaningful information about your emotions, beliefs and behavior. Turning your perfectionism 'on' or 'off' and seeing the consequences is a great way to gather important information about what way of behaving works best for *you*. Such information enables you to have choices and, ultimately, freedom.

Now, using the example of a completed behavioral experiment in Box 7.4.2 for guidance, set up your own behavioral experiment using Worksheet 7.4.1.

BOX 7.4.2 AN EXAMPLE OF A BEHAVIORAL EXPERIMENT

1. Belief: I must keep my house perfectly tidy at all times.

2. Identify prediction(s) in general: If my house is not clean and tidy, people will think I am lazy and dirty. I will be extremely embarrassed.

3. Specify the prediction: My friend will show clearly that she is disgusted by staring at the mess and dirt, avoiding eye contact, commenting on the mess and not relaxing. I will feel embarrassed and anxious (intensity ratings: 90 per cent and 75 per cent), will make excuses for the mess and will not enjoy myself (belief rating: 100 per cent).

4. Experiment: Invite a friend to visit; deliberately leave dirty dishes in the sink, and don't vacuum before she arrives.

5. Results: The friend visited and did not even look at the washing or floor. She did not avoid eye contact but chatted as usual. I did feel anxious (65 per cent) and made excuses for the mess. However, my friend said she too rarely managed to keep on top of everything. The anxiety was less severe than anticipated, and reduced rapidly within the first half-hour of the friend's visit. I was surprised to discover that I enjoyed myself.

6. Reflection: I not only enjoyed the visit, I also appreciated not having to spend hours beforehand cleaning. I was interested to learn that my friend's house is not always tidy. I concluded that my perfectionism did not necessarily help me to enjoy entertaining but actually made it more stressful.

7. Revised belief: I should try to keep my house reasonably tidy most of the time, but the odd bit of mess doesn't matter.

WORKSHEET 7.4.1: BEHAVIORAL EXPERIMENT

1. Belief:

2. Identify the prediction in general:

3: Specify the prediction precisely (specify behaviors and rate intensity of beliefs and emotions):

4. Experiment:

5. Results:

6. Reflection:

7. Revised belief:

What did you find by completing a behavioral experiment? Hopefully you will have gained new information about the unhelpful predictions you were making about your perfectionism.

Keep going with behavioral experiments. The key is to try to 'shake up' beliefs that have not been working for you – to test out the way you have been seeing the world until now to see whether some of your predictions are in fact true or not. Try some of the ideas for behavioral experiments in Box 7.4.3, which attack some common perfectionist predictions.

BOX 7.4.3 EXAMPLES OF PERFECTIONIST BELIEFS AND PREDICTIONS THAT CAN USEFULLY BE TESTED IN BEHAVIORAL EXPERIMENTS

Belief/prediction	Experiment
Belief: I'll do better if I work hard. *Prediction:* I'll get A if I work hard, B if I work moderately and I'll fail if I don't work at all.	Work excessively hard for one piece of work, moderately for another and minimally for a third. Is the outcome as you predicted?
Belief: If I don't come top, I'll feel like a failure for ages. *Prediction:* I'll feel anxious, miserable and think that I am a failure as a person all day, every day, for at least a week.	Deliberately don't come top in something trivial (e.g. a running race with a friend down the street). Is the outcome as you predicted? Build up to testing the prediction in more meaningful/important situations.
Belief: If I start something, I have to finish it completely. *Prediction:* If I leave something half-done, it will prey on my mind (100 per cent) and I won't be able to sleep for more than a couple of hours.	Leave something half-finished. Does it prey on your mind? How much? For how long? Did you sleep? For how long?

Belief: If I don't take everything with me on a weekend away, I might have the wrong clothes and will have to come home.
Prediction: If I don't bring lots of different choices, I will worry about it (100 per cent) and will end up coming home.

Leave just one item behind. What happens to your worry? Did you end up coming home? Can you build up to packing fewer clothes?

Belief: If I don't write everything down, I'll make lots of serious mistakes.
Prediction: If I don't write down everything I need to do today, I'll forget something important like giving my daughter her medicine.

Leave one thing off a list (such as your daughter's medicine). Did you remember it? What was it like not writing it down? Can you write a shorter list with just very important things on it? How many mistakes do you make?

Belief: Training hard makes me happy because it is the right thing to do and I achieve more.
Prediction: I'm happier when I train hard than when I don't and I will win more races.

Train hard for one week – really push yourself. How happy does it make you (0–10)? How unhappy does it make you (0–100)? What else do you observe? How did you do? Don't train as hard for a week and make the same notes. Compare the results.

Final comment

There is no 'right' behavioral experiment and you should be spending time doing many experiments to test a whole range of beliefs. Gradually you will gather information about the reality of a variety of situations. That in turn will lead you to some conclusions about how to live a happier, more relaxed, more fulfilling life where success and achievement are balanced with enjoyment and relaxation.

TAKE-HOME MESSAGE

- Behavioral experiments are used to gather information about your beliefs, emotions and behaviors.
- The results of the experiments will give you personalized, meaningful information about your beliefs and behaviors associated with perfectionism.
- The information from the experiments should be added to the growing pile of information you are gathering about reality and should help you on your way to a more balanced, happier way of living.

7.5 From 'all or nothing thinking' to flexibility and freedom

Remember Chapter 4, when we outlined what keeps perfectionism going? Many of these factors relate to how perfectionism involves setting rigid rules and standards, and evaluating compliance with these rules using a thinking style called 'all or nothing thinking'. It is also known as 'black and white thinking'. All or nothing thinking involves judging things in terms of absolutes, using polar opposite categories: so something is either 'good' or 'bad', 'right' or 'wrong', a 'complete failure' or a 'complete success'. The main problem in perfectionism is that a person sets very rigid rules about the standards that they expect themselves to reach, and judges their own performance through all or nothing thinking. Because the rules and standards are so rigid and difficult to achieve (e.g. I must never eat a piece of chocolate; I must always achieve above 80 per cent) often the person fails to achieve them, and then judges that this means that they are a 'complete' failure (e.g. because they ate one piece of chocolate, or got a mark of 79 per cent for an assignment). What is more, when a person *does* reach their standard, instead of thinking they are a 'complete success' when they meet their rigid standard (e.g. not eating chocolate, or receiving 80 per cent for an assignment), they are in fact likely to discount having reached this goal as too easy, and re-set the rule even higher (e.g. never eating any high-fat foods, receiving above 85 per cent for assignments).

In Section 7.4 we introduced the technique of using behavioral experiments to test your predictions. In this section we will focus first on changing all or nothing thinking, which is a core part of what keeps perfectionism going, and second on how to replace rigid rules and standards with guidelines and ways to increase being flexible in thoughts and behaviors.

All or nothing thinking

This thinking style, which is particularly prominent in perfectionism, is described as follows:

> *All or nothing thinking involves judging standards in two categories, and viewing things in extremes, for example: 'good or bad', 'failed or achieved', 'complete or incomplete', 'always or never', 'totally or not at all'.*

All or nothing thinking is also referred to as 'dichotomous thinking'. Dichotomous thinking was identified as a central part of what keeps perfectionism going in the model developed at Oxford University, and a research study by Sarah Egan and her colleagues at Curtin University in Australia found that it was one important factor that distinguished between positive striving for achievement and unhelpful perfectionism. So if you judge whether you meet your standards using all or nothing thinking, it is likely to lead to problems.

The problem with all or nothing thinking is that it leaves no room for the middle ground or shades of gray. Judging your own performance using all or nothing thinking means that there is no place for 'average' performance between these categories of having failed or achieved a standard. Some examples of all or nothing thinking can be seen in Box 7.5.1.

BOX 7.5.1 EXAMPLES OF ALL OR NOTHING THINKING IN AREAS OF PERFECTIONISM

Area	Example of all or nothing thinking
Eating/weight/shape	If I eat one chocolate biscuit, then I have completely failed If I weigh 51 kg, and not my perfect goal weight of 50 kg, I have completely failed
Work	If I cannot get the whole report finished today, I might as well not even start it
Study	If I do not get a distinction grade, I am a complete failure
Appearance	If I do not have my shirt ironed exactly perfect with no creases, my colleagues will think I am completely lazy
House cleanliness	If I do not clean the floors every day, then the house is always dirty
Hygiene	Unless my hands feel perfectly clean, they are completely dirty and I need to wash them again
Sport	Unless I win Athlete of the Year, I might as well give up trying
Parenting	If I ever get even slightly angry with my child, this shows I am a completely bad parent

Two tools can be useful to help overcome your all or nothing thinking: they are *behavioral experiments* and *continuums*.

Overcoming all or nothing thinking with behavioral experiments

You know from the previous section how to create behavioral experiments. These can be really useful in overcoming all or nothing thinking. Remember the case of Simon in Chapter 2, who would procrastinate over cleaning his house? Box 7.5.2 shows an example of how Simon was able to devise a behavioral experiment to test his all or nothing thinking about cleaning.

BOX 7.5.2 AN EXAMPLE OF A BEHAVIORAL EXPERIMENT TO TEST ALL OR NOTHING THINKING ABOUT CLEANING

1. **All or nothing belief:** Unless I have my whole house clean and ordered there is no point having friends over.

2. **Identify my prediction:** If my entire house is not perfectly clean and ordered, people will think I am completely lazy and dirty.

3. **Specify the prediction precisely (rate 0–100 per cent):** Unless the house is perfect I will be very embarrassed if I invite a friend over as she will think I am lazy and dirty. She will stare at the mess and tease me, saying that I am not as organized and clean as she thought I would be. I will feel embarrassed (90 per cent) and not enjoy myself (100 per cent).

4. **Experiment:** Start overcoming my procrastination about cleaning by doing only the kitchen, leaving all of the other rooms disorganized and not clean by my standard, then invite my friend Samantha to visit.

5. **Results:** Samantha visited but did not stare at the other rooms. I felt a little embarrassed (40 per cent) when she glanced at the other rooms but she did not tease me. I enjoyed myself (80 per cent), having coffee and a good chat with her.

> **6. Reflection:** I did not have to clean the entire house; I was able to get started by doing just one room. I enjoyed having a friend over and she did not tease me for having a messy house.

> **7. Revised belief:** I do not have to do things either completely perfectly or not at all. Just starting one thing can help, and having done this I was more relaxed (75 per cent).

You can see from Simon's example that a major part of what was driving his avoidance and procrastination about cleaning his house was all or nothing thinking, and that he was able to challenge this effectively through a behavioral experiment.

Now try doing a behavioral experiment for your all or nothing thinking by completing Worksheet 7.5.1. Another example of how to do this is included in Box 7.5.3, showing the worksheet for Tony, a 29-year-old electrician who was renovating his apartment at weekends, and recently painted his lounge room and feels very dissatisfied and anxious about the results. His behavioral experiment was a mixture of an 'experiment' and a survey. As we said before, there are no rules about what is 'right' and what is 'wrong'. The goal is to gather the information you need to test the validity of your beliefs.

BOX 7.5.3 TONY'S WORKSHEET, TESTING ALL OR NOTHING BELIEFS WITH A BEHAVIORAL EXPERIMENT

1. My all or nothing belief: Because there are a few small smudges of paint on the ceiling from painting the wall, the whole lounge room painting job is ruined.

2. My prediction: Other people will think I am hopeless at tasks around the house and have done a bad job of the painting.

3. Specify the prediction precisely: People will comment that the smudges really stand out (85 per cent) and express dissatisfaction with the overall effect. I will feel anxious (70 per cent).

4. Experiment: Conduct a survey of people to see what they think of the painting.

5. Results: No one said they could particularly notice the smudges and that they liked the painting.

6. Reflection: Because of my perfectionism I focus in on tiny flaws that others do not notice.

7. Revised belief: Small imperfections in a task around the house do not mean the job is completely ruined (65 per cent).

Now you have completed a behavioral experiment for your all or nothing thinking, what have you concluded as a result? Often in therapy people are surprised to find that even though they have been judging things in all or nothing categories for a long time, by changing the way they do things, and not accepting these categories, they can start to feel to feel more relaxed, and be more flexible in their thinking. One of the keys to combating all or nothing thinking is to complete numerous behavioral experiments, so keep using Worksheet 7.5.1 with different all or nothing thoughts (there is a blank version of the worksheet at the back of the book that you can copy as many times as you need). The more you practice changing your all or nothing thinking, the easier it will become.

Overcoming all or nothing thinking with fancy lines

Another tool that can be used to overcome all or nothing thinking is to think about performance in terms of a

WORKSHEET 7.5.1: TESTING ALL OR NOTHING BELIEFS WITH A BEHAVIORAL EXPERIMENT

1. Identify your all or nothing belief

2. Identify your prediction in general

3. Specify your prediction precisely (specify behaviors and rate intensity of beliefs and emotions)

4. Create an experiment to test your all or nothing belief

5. Record the results of the experiment

6. Reflection: what have you learned from the experiment?

7. Devise a revised belief

'continuum', which for our purposes is a fancy name for a continuous line between two opposite extremes. This technique can help a person to see that their performance does not in fact fall into one of two opposite categories (e.g. *'If I am not the very best, I am a complete failure'*), but that there are shades of gray between these black and white categories.

To help you understand continuums we will use the case of Ifioma, who was introduced in Chapter 2. Ifioma had perfectionism in two main areas of her life; eating/shape/weight and work. Ifioma had examples of all or nothing thinking in relation to her work, where she thought she either worked excessively for several weeks in a row and achieved a lot, or didn't do any work at all and achieved nothing. In Box 7.5.4 you can see an example of a completed continuum form for Ifioma.

BOX 7.5.4 EXAMPLE OF USING A CONTINUUM TO CHALLENGE ALL OR NOTHING THINKING ABOUT WORK

Step 1. Identify the all or nothing thought

Step 2. Specify the all or nothing categories on the continuum

Step 3. Think of examples when there are different points along the continuum

Step 4. Reflect on what I learned from the continuum

1. What is my all or nothing thought?
I either work excessively for several weeks, when I am able to achieve a lot of work, or abandon work altogether for several weeks and get nothing done at all.

2. Specify the all or nothing categories on the continuum
No work _____ Extreme work

3. Examples of points along the continuum in the thought/behavior (is it truly the case that it is completely all or nothing?)

Attending team meeting when I was feeling slack at work and did not prepare as much as I would like, but I still went and was able to contribute a few ideas.

No work _____X_____ Extreme work

Working many hours preparing presentation for team meeting, which left me feeling exhausted for two days after, although I could have actually worked harder

No work _____X____ Extreme work

Feeling overwhelmed and so anxious that I could not start preparing a presentation until my colleague Fiona helped me.

No work ___X_____ Extreme work

4. What I learned from the continuums

When I consider specific examples I can see that there are different points along the continuum and that there are shades of gray in my work behavior, so it is not true that I either completely work or do none at all.

It can be seen from Ifioma's example that completing a continuum form was helpful in getting her to think about her work performance along a continuum rather than in all or nothing categories. This enabled her to think more flexibly, and to discover that in fact her behavior at work did not fall into the opposite categories of either working with complete intensity or not working at all.

To help you to gain more flexibility and reconsider your all or nothing thoughts, look at Box 7.5.5, which gives you another example of how Ifioma was able to challenge an all or nothing thought – this time about eating – and then complete Worksheet 7.5.2.

> ## BOX 7.5.5 IFIOMA'S WORKSHEET: TESTING ALL OR NOTHING THINKING WITH CONTINUUMS
>
> **1. What is my all or nothing thought?** If I eat one piece of chocolate I have completely failed at my diet and will not be able to stop eating it.
>
> **2. Specify the all or nothing categories on the continuum**
> Stick perfectly to diet/Completely abandon diet
>
> **3. Example of when there are points along the continuum in the thought/behavior** (is it truly the case that it is completely all or nothing?)
> Last week I ate a few pieces of chocolate at my friend's house but did not continue to overeat on chocolate
> Stick perfectly to diet _____X____ Completely abandon diet
>
> **4. What I learned from the continuums:** I can eat one piece of chocolate now and then and not always overeat. I do not have to keep all or nothing rules about food

What did you find out when you completed Worksheet 7.5.2? Were you able to challenge your all or nothing thoughts by identifying examples when there were shades of gray in your behavior – that it was not in fact completely all or nothing?

There are other books about how to use continua.* Typical continua have 'good' and 'bad' at either end. It can also be helpful to think about other people you know who are neither good nor bad, neither fat nor thin, neither completely successful nor complete failures but somewhere in between.

Having introduced two main tools in overcoming all or nothing thinking in perfectionism, using behavioral

---

*One good one is Padesky and Greenberger's *Mind Over Mood*, and the associated website: for details see the 'References and further reading' section at the back of this book.

WORKSHEET 7.5.2: TESTING ALL OR NOTHING THINKING WITH CONTINUUMS

1. What is my all or nothing thought?

2. Specify the all or nothing categories on the continuum

3. Examples of when there are points along the continuum in the thought/behavior (is it truly the case that it is completely all or nothing?)

Example 1:

Example 2:

Example 3:

4. What I learned from the continuum:

experiments and lines to help increase your flexibility in thinking and behavior, we now turn to considering further how to increase flexibility, and how to gain a sense of freedom by replacing *rules* for behavior with *guidelines*.

Turning rigid rules into guidelines: The path to flexibility and freedom

People with perfectionism set themselves very rigid and demanding rules by which they measure their performance. The problem with this is that a person who sets themselves rigid, all or nothing rules (e.g. I must get over 80 per cent in all my marks or I am a complete failure) can become trapped in a cycle of all or nothing evaluation of their goals. The person is likely either to think that they have completely failed at something (e.g. receiving 79 per cent), or, when they do achieve their standard (e.g. receiving 80 per cent), they either discount it or to re-set their standard even higher (e.g. I must get above 85 per cent because 80 per cent is not that good). So having rigid rules in judging how well you are doing at your standards is a no-win situation. Here we outline two ways to help change this vicious cycle: replacing rules with guidelines and accepting less than perfect performance.

Replacing rules with guidelines: Becoming flexible

It is helpful to start to identify the particular rules that you have for your performance, and aim to replace these rules with guidelines instead. To use Christopher Fairburn's distinction, 'rules break, guidelines bend.' This means that you might replace a rigid rule such as 'I must never eat chocolate' with instead a guideline that 'I aim to eat healthily and not to eat chocolate every day, but if I eat it now and then it is OK.'

The first step is to list all of your 'rules', your 'musts' and your 'shoulds'. Here is Fatima's list, which took her about two minutes to generate:

I MUST ALWAYS

Brush my teeth twice a day	Put my hand in front of my mouth when yawning	Ensure that I do some exercise every day
Comb my hair twice a day	Say 'bless you' when others sneeze	Make sure that I never go above the recommended weekly alcohol intake
Make the bed after I get up	Answer the phone when it rings	Draw the curtains at home
Flush the toilet after using it	Unplug all electrical appliances at night	Phone my mother-in-law at least once a week
Pick up my clothes from the floor	Return phone calls within 24 hours	Put my photographs in an album
Be polite	Back up my computer with a memory stick	Check the oil level in the car
Consider others	Put other people before myself	Shred all my personal documents that could identify me
Do something to 'better' myself each day	Eat less than 1,500 calories a day	Plan ahead and be organized

Read useful literature and not trash	Remember other people's birthdays	Make sure there is food in the fridge
Eat five portions of fruit and vegetables per day	Keep my office looking nice	Do something productive each day

Even prisoners get time off for good behavior and eventually get parole. Do you get time off? Do you get parole from the prison of rules and regulations that you are building around you? No harm will come if the rule about eating five portions of fruit and vegetables per day is turned into a guideline, if you sometimes read a trashy magazine, and if you don't check the oil level on the car one day. If you forget someone's birthday no harm will be done, and there is no danger from leaving your clothes on the floor (with the exception of shoes in doorways because someone may trip over them). Don't take our word for it. Try it yourself – and use behavioral experiments to turn your rules into guidelines. Here are some suggestions.

Behavioral experiments aimed at doing things less than perfectly

One way to relax your rules and turn them into guidelines is to create experiments aimed at doing things less than perfectly, that is, just doing them well enough, rather than to a perfect standard. To help you to do this, look at Box 7.5.6, which records a behavioral experiment undertaken by Maggie, a 32-year-old receptionist who has perfectionism about her appearance. Then complete Worksheet 7.5.3, choosing a perfectionist belief of your own and conducting an experiment to challenge the rule.

BOX 7.5.6 MAGGIE'S WORKSHEET: A BEHAVIORAL EXPERIMENT IN DOING THINGS LESS THAN PERFECTLY

What is my perfectionist belief? Others will not like me unless I am always perfectly well groomed and present myself well.

Identify the prediction in general: If I do not have a perfect appearance my friends will comment and criticize me.

Specify the prediction precisely (with ratings from 0–100 per cent) Unless I have absolutely perfect make-up and hair when I go out, my friends will think I have completely let myself go and that I am lazy by commenting that I look bad (90 per cent). I will feel very anxious (95 per cent).

Experiment: Meet friends for coffee with messy hair and no make-up.

Results: Friends did not comment that I looked bad. I felt more relaxed – one friend said I was looking more relaxed than she had seen me in a long time.

Reflection: I learned from the experiment that I do not need to have a completely perfect appearance; friends accept me as I am and don't think about my appearance.

Revised belief: My friends are more interested in spending time with me than in scrutinizing me to see if I have perfect hair and make-up (70 per cent).

WORKSHEET 7.5.3: DOING THINGS LESS THAN PERFECTLY WITH A
BEHAVIORAL EXPERIMENT

What is my perfectionist belief?

Identify the prediction in general:

Specify the prediction precisely (with ratings from 0–100 per cent):

Experiment:

Results:

Reflection:

Revised belief:

You can see from Box 7.5.6 that through a behavioral experiment Maggie was able to relax her rule that she must always have a perfect appearance, and learned that she felt more relaxed and others accepted her when she was not following this rigid rule. As a result, Maggie was able to change her rule into a guideline – that while she likes to take care of her appearance, she does not need to have it perfect, and that others accept her whether she is perfectly groomed or casual in her appearance.

What did you find from completing Worksheet 7.5.3? Were you able to create an experiment involving doing things less than perfectly? There are many ways for you to do things less than perfectly – the trick is to identify the particular rules that you have made for yourself, and keep doing behavioral experiments in which you test what happens when you do things less than perfectly. For example, if you have a rule that you must only ever take a perfectly baked cake to someone's house, then try taking a cake that is slightly lopsided; or if you have a rule that you must always file things perfectly before leaving the office, try leaving one day without doing the filing.

Behavioral experiments aimed at reducing the amount of time spent on a task

Another way to replace your rules with guidelines is to reduce the amount of time you allocate to tasks. Again, you can use behavioral experiments to test what the effect of this is. Many people in therapy are dubious about the idea of doing this – for example, spending only three hours preparing a report rather than their usual ten hours; however, often after doing behavioral experiments they are surprised to learn that they get similar results, whether in study grades, work performance or artistic/sporting endeavours, even when they spend less time on the task. This is because often when someone is having trouble with perfectionism, they are spending a lot of time feeling anxious or engaging in counter-productive behaviors (e.g. reading a paragraph over and over). Look at Box 7.5.7, which shows an example of a behavioral experiment for the case of Suzie, who, as we saw in Chapter 3, was very worried about not doing a good job as a physiotherapist and would spend many hours completing case notes so that she could provide the best possible service to her clients. Then try a similar experiment for yourself, using Worksheet 7.5.4.

BOX 7.5.7 SUZIE'S WORKSHEET: A BEHAVIORAL EXPERIMENT ON REDUCING THE AMOUNT OF TIME SPENT ON A TASK

What is my perfectionist belief? I must always be completely thorough in my work

Identify the prediction in general: I must spend 4 hours after work writing my case notes or I might miss something and my clients will be dissatisfied with me

Specify the prediction precisely (with ratings from 0–100 per cent): If I spend only 1 hour writing my case notes, I will miss something and clients will complain during the week about my service (80 per cent)

Experiment: Spend one week writing case notes for only one hour after work each night, rather than four hours

Results: No clients complained about my service – in fact there was no difference in how I treated my clients and they were as usual saying how much I help them

Reflections: I learned that I do not have to spend so long writing my case notes; in fact, I was wasting my time spending four hours writing notes

Revised belief: I have a good knowledge of my field and I am unlikely to miss things even if I spend less time writing my case notes (80 per cent)

WORKSHEET 7.5.4: REDUCING THE AMOUNT OF TIME SPENT ON A TASK WITH A BEHAVIORAL EXPERIMENT

What is my perfectionist belief?

Identify the prediction in general:

Specify the prediction precisely (with ratings from 0–100 per cent):

Experiment:

Results:

Reflection:

Revised belief:

What did you learn by completing Worksheet 7.5.4 and reducing the amount of time you are spending on tasks in pursuit of your high standards and perfect performance? Many people are very surprised to learn that they can get the same results as they did before with less time. The positive benefit from relaxing rules about time spent is that you feel less anxious and have more time to get your life better balanced – for example, engaging in leisure activities if you have been spending excessive amounts of time at work. Again, as with the behavioral experiments aimed at doing things less than perfectly, it is useful to keep repeating these experiments often to reduce the amount of time you are spending on meeting high standards.

Freedom from rules: Accepting less than perfect performance

A final way to free oneself from the constraints of rule-based, all or nothing thinking is to consider accepting less than perfect performance. Think back to Chapter 6, where you considered the costs and benefits of perfectionism in your life. To overcome perfectionism so that its negative impacts in one's life – fatigue, anxiety, never having enough time – are reduced, one has to be willing, at least to some degree, to accept not being completely satisfied with one's performance. Striving is often a way to achieve a sense of self-esteem; however, as we will discuss in more detail in Chapter 9, basing one's sense of self on striving can be very problematic.

Becoming more flexible and free will involve your learning to accept in a positive way that performance cannot always be perfect, and that to have a more balanced life you may need to accept a level of performance with which you might not be entirely happy. For example, take the case of Chloe, who has been a perfectionist about her work as a surgeon and her sport of running. In order to be more flexible and have balance in her life she is now willing to accept less than perfect performance in both of these areas, so that she experiences less anxiety and has time for other things in life such as socializing. For example, it would be very difficult for Chloe to be the top surgeon in her hospital, or to win every running event she entered. By accepting that she can be a good surgeon and a good runner, but does not need to be the very best surgeon or unbeatable in her races, Chloe is making a positive choice to have more balance in her life. Acceptance of less than perfect performance is a sign of someone who is able to be strong and wise in choosing a balanced life, rather than being passively resigned to an unhappy fate.

We suggest that you consider accepting that your performance cannot always be perfect and relaxing your rule-based thinking. Doing this will increase your ability to think and behave in a flexible way, help you achieve more balance in your life, and offer you a sense of freedom from these rigid rules. We will return to this topic in more detail in Chapter 10 on 'freedom'.

TAKE-HOME MESSAGE

- All or nothing thinking involves judging your performance in categorical terms. It is a major part of what keeps perfectionism going and can be overcome by doing behavioral experiments and using continuums.
- Flexibility can be increased by replacing rules with guidelines by doing things less than perfectly and reducing the amount of time spent on tasks.
- Acceptance of less than perfect performance can help increase flexibility and give you a sense of balance and freedom in life.

7.6 Learning to notice the positive

In the previous section, we suggested how you can overcome all or nothing thinking. In this chapter we will look at another common thinking style in perfectionism: paying attention only, or mainly, to negative information about performance and discounting positive information.

Noticing negative aspects of performance

One of the problems in perfectionism is that people become selectively attuned to noticing any negative aspects of their performance, no matter how small the perceived flaw may be. They constantly monitor their performance, like a judge, constantly looking out for evidence that something is not quite right, not quite up to scratch. This scrutiny can involve focusing on even very small details or perceived shortcomings. We saw an example of this style of thinking in Tony (Section 7.5), who was excessively concerned about very small flaws in the painting job he did in his apartment. We can also see this focus on the negative in Aimee (Chapter 2), who was perfectionist about entertaining guests. She spent many hours cleaning before having guests over for dinner and as a result had limited time available to make the food and ended up making a lopsided dessert; she focused in on this and thought it was a bad mistake. At the dinner party itself, Aimee found it very difficult to focus on her friends' conversation because she was thinking excessively about having made an error in the dessert, and afterwards she was plagued by thoughts that she had ruined the event by making a defective dessert and had failed as a host. Thus, she was selectively concentrating on a minor flaw in perform-ance, and as a result noticing only the negative, while ignoring or discounting the many positive aspects to the event. For example, she did not reflect on the fact that everyone had a good time and said all of the food was delicious – indeed, people even commented that the cake tasted good. If you were to survey the guests at Aimee's dinner party on her performance as a host, what would you guess they would say? Of course, they would say that she had not failed: on the contrary, she had made a very nice meal and everyone had had an enjoyable time. So in reality the fact that the dessert was lopsided made no difference.

The basic problem here is that when one regularly scrutinizes performance critically and focuses in on any negative point, one can end up minimizing or entirely ignoring any success in performance and so coming to a generally critical conclusion about oneself.

There are several ways to overcome this 'noticing the negative' thinking style, including becoming aware of the areas where one scrutinizes performance, and broadening one's attention.

Where do you scrutinize your performance?

One of the key aspects of this 'noticing the negative' thinking style is that attention is focused on flaws in performance in areas that are important to the person. This is not surprising, since people often focus their attention on things that are personally relevant to them. For example, have you ever bought a new car? If so, in the week after buying the car, did you suddenly start to notice many more cars that were similar to your own? That is, similar colored cars and similar models? Is it the case that there were actually more cars similar to yours on the road the week after you bought yours? Most of us would agree that is unlikely – what happened is that, because in the week after buying your car you are thinking about it and it is important to you, you started to notice similar cars. Another example is when a woman finds out she is pregnant, and suddenly she starts to notice babies everywhere, baby-related items at the super-market, and so on, because this area has become personally important to her, then attention is focused on it.

The same principle applies with 'noticing the negative' in perfectionism. Some examples of noticing the negative in common areas of perfectionism are given in Box 7.6.1.

BOX 7.6.1 EXAMPLES OF 'NOTICING THE NEGATIVE' IN DIFFERENT AREAS OF PERFECTIONISM

Area	Example of 'noticing the negative'
Work	My performance at work is poor because I made two spelling errors in the report
Appearance	I looked a mess because I had a small hole in my tights
House cleanliness	The house is not clean because there are a few streaks on the windows
Study	I performed poorly in the oral presentation because I mispronounced one or two words
Eating/shape/weight	Even though I am a size 8 my body shape is too big overall because my thighs are too large
Sport	Even though I was placed in the race, my performance was poor as I did not start as quickly as I should have

Intimate relationships	I do not have a good relationship with my partner because we argue sometimes
Social performance	I made a fool of myself because I stumbled over my words at one point in the conversation
Hygiene	I will spread germs to people because I have a small cut on my hand
Parenting	I am a bad parent because my child only says 'please' and 'thank you' about 75 per cent of the time when we are out

One of the reasons why this thinking style keeps going is that the more someone pays attention to their performance in a particular area, the more they think about this area and the more important it becomes to them: so continually focusing on the negative aspects maintains a preoccupation with performance in the area.

To set about overcoming this thinking style, start by completing Worksheet 7.6.1 to become aware of when you are focusing your attention on flaws and noticing the negative; then try *at the time this happens* to broaden your attention. For some guidance, see Box 7.6.2, which shows how Aimee could do this.

BOX 7.6.2 AIMEE'S WORKSHEET: NOTICING THE NEGATIVE AND BROADENING ATTENTION

Step 1. Identify the area of perfectionism.

Step 2. Record the negative thoughts as you notice them, and rate how strongly you believe them on a scale of 0–100 per cent.

Step 3. Identify ways to broaden your attention to include *all* of the information. Ask yourself: (a) What positive aspects of my

performance am I missing? (b) How can I focus my attention on things other than negative flaws, e.g. on noticing details around me?
Step 4. Record the outcome of broadening your attention.

1. Identify the area of perfectionism: Entertaining

2. Record negative thoughts and rate strength of belief in them: The fact that I made a lopsided dessert means I am a bad host (90 per cent)

3. Ways to broaden my attention in the situation: (a) I am ignoring that people said the food was good and they had fun; (b) I can focus on conversations, ask friends questions and notice details around me (e.g. color of my friends' outfits)

4. Outcome: When I consider the evidence, the dinner was a success overall. Focusing on conversation and colors broadens my attention.

What did you find as a result of completing Worksheet 7.6.1? Was it surprising to see that you are ignoring many positive aspects of your performance and paying a great deal of attention only to negative aspects? It is important to keep practicing this skill by completing numerous records to try to broaden your attention. It is best if you can try to broaden your attention *at the time* that you are noticing the negative thoughts. It can be difficult sometimes to acknowledge the positive aspects of your performance at the time, and this is where learning to focus on other aspects of the situation can be really helpful in drawing your attention away from any negative points. So, for example, when you are talking to a colleague at work, rather than dwelling on the negative thought that your appearance is flawed because you have a crease in your shirt, broaden your attention to focus on the content of what your colleague is saying, what the color of his shirt is and what objects are around you at

WORKSHEET 7.6.1: NOTICING THE NEGATIVE AND BROADENING ATTENTION

Step 1. Identify the area of perfectionism.

Step 2. Record the negative thoughts as you notice them, and rate how strongly you believe them on a scale of 0–100 per cent.

Step 3. Identify ways to broaden your attention to include *all* of the information. Ask yourself: (a) What positive aspects of my performance am I missing? (b) How can I focus my attention on things other than negative flaws, e.g. on noticing details around me?

Step 4. Record the outcome of broadening your attention.

1. Identify the area of perfectionism

2. Record negative thoughts and rate strength of belief in them

3. Ways to broaden my attention in the situation

4. Outcome

Reflection on Worksheet 7.6.1:
What did you learn about your perfectionism by completing this worksheet?

the time, and asking him questions about his weekend. If you are having trouble broadening your attention in the situation, try actively to bring your attention into the moment by focusing on the content of what you see and hear, and involve yourself in what is going on around you, rather than what is going on inside your head.

Discounting positive aspects of performance and raising the bar

So far in this section we have been focusing on how in perfectionism one continually monitors and notices negative aspects of performance. Another thinking style that goes along with this is discounting positive aspects of performance – as, for example, when Aimee discounted the evidence that people liked the food she had prepared. Discounting the positive also occurs in how someone with perfectionism reacts to meeting a standard. For example, common thoughts that occur in perfectionism when a goal is reached are:

It was not that hard
Anyone could have done that
It was no big deal
If I can achieve this goal, it's too easy; I need to make it harder next time

Someone who discounts all the positive aspects of their performance, and whenever they reach a goal re-sets it at a higher level, is putting themselves in a no-win situation of feeling that they are always failing in their performance. Re-setting standards is particularly unhelpful and a sure-fire way to feel miserable. Take a moment to think back about whether you have re-set your standards on achieving a goal? Why did you do that? Was it a helpful strategy? Could you conduct a behavioral experiment to see whether keeping the same standard if you meet it actually works better in your life, reduces emotional distress and gives you an increased sense of self-worth?

If you have spent a great deal of time in your life noticing the negative aspects of your performance and discounting the positive aspects, it takes a conscious effort to start to record *actual* evidence of performance in situations, to help redress the balance. To help you to do this, keep a diary of events over a week, and record in Worksheet 7.6.2 anything positive with regard to your performance, and the absence of any negative comments about performance. A few examples are given at the top of Worksheet 7.6.2 to help get you started.

What did you find out by keeping this diary? Hopefully it helped you begin to notice positive aspects of your performance, and the lack of negative evidence. The key to using this tool is practice. Because you have probably had a longstanding habit of discounting positive success, you need to search actively for evidence of the positives, and for evidence for the lack of negative aspects. Eventually you will get into a new habit in thinking in which you notice all the aspects of your performance in a more balanced way. Because this takes a lot of practice, it will be helpful if you continue to keep this diary over several weeks until you really start to notice the positive aspects of performance and the lack of negative aspects more automatically.

Another helpful way to challenge noticing the negative and discounting the positive is to use cognitive restructuring: we will cover this tool in Section 7.7.

WORKSHEET 7.6.2: DIARY OF POSITIVE COMMENTS AND LACK OF
NEGATIVE COMMENTS

Area	Positive evidence	Lack of negative evidence
Work	Boss commented that I did a good job on my presentation	No one criticized the presentation or how I appeared
Appearance	Friend commented that I looked good tonight	No one said that I looked bad
Social	People approached me to talk	No one said I looked anxious or that I was boring

Reflection on Worksheet 7.6.2:
What did you learn about your perfectionism by completing this
worksheet?

TAKE-HOME MESSAGE

- In perfectionism a thinking style of noticing the negative aspects of performance keeps the problem going.
- Often this thinking style goes along with another which involves discounting positive aspects of performance, and discounting success when goals are reached.
- Broadening your attention in the situation when you are noticing the negative can be useful.
- Recording a diary of positive aspects of performance, and lack of negative comments about performance, can help to change these unhelpful thinking styles.

7.7 Changing thinking styles

The previous two sections have shown you some ways to change all or nothing thinking, noticing the negative and discounting the positive. In this section we will continue along these lines in looking at how to challenge other common thinking styles in perfectionism, including having double standards, saying 'should' to yourself, and over-generalization. We will also consider how to tackle any type of unhelpful thinking through the process of *cognitive restructuring*, which is a tool to help change negative thoughts.

The impact of thinking on feelings and behavior

In previous chapters we have looked at ways to change thinking, using behavioral experiments and other tools to help overcome negative thinking. The reason why it is important to become aware of what you are thinking is that when we you have a negative thought about yourself, such as 'I am a failure' or 'I am not good enough', this has a strong impact on the way you feel.

Consider a situation where two students each receive a mark of 79 per cent for their exam. The first student, without perfectionism, thinks that this is a good result, which although not a distinction is still a very good grade, and so feels happy. The second student, with perfectionism, thinks that this result has fallen short of their standard of always getting distinctions, and that this means they are a failure, and so as a result feels depressed and anxious. So two people can be in exactly the same situation and yet have opposite emotional reactions: one feels happy, and the other depressed. What is accounting for the difference in the way they feel?

The answer is that they feel differently because they are thinking differently. What we say to ourselves and what we think has a profound impact on our mood. When you have perfectionism and are often thinking that you are failing, or criticizing yourself for not doing well enough, this way of thinking makes you feel anxious and depressed.

Not only does negative thinking have an impact on your feelings, it also has an impact on the way you behave. For example, if you are thinking before going to a party that you might not know what to say and that no one will like you, you are likely to feel very anxious and then might avoid going to the party. Or if you're thinking that you would never be able to make a perfect meal to serve to guests, you might never invite friends over for dinner.

So it is important to become aware of what you are thinking, because negative thinking can have a very unhelpful impact on your feelings and your behavior. Because it is so important to realize your habitual thinking patterns, in the next sections we list some more common unhelpful thinking styles, beginning with those especially often found with perfectionism. Read through these and see if you recognize any that apply to you.

Common thinking styles in perfectionism

Double standards

One of the styles of thinking that keeps perfectionism going is holding double standards. This is where you have one set of harsh standards for yourself and another set of more lenient standards for others. For example, you may think that it is OK for others to make small errors, for example, a spelling mistake in an email, but not OK for you to make a spelling mistake in an email. The double standard is that you accept that others can make small mistakes but see it as unacceptable for yourself. Aimee had a set of double standards about entertaining: she believed that if there was a small flaw in a meal cooked by someone else this was just normal, but that if it happened in a meal that she had cooked it was not acceptable.

It can be useful when you are doing cognitive restructuring (which we shall come on to later in this section) to examine whether one of the themes in your thinking is holding double standards. If you do hold double standards, try doing a survey to find out what other people's standards are. Ask people you know whether they also hold double standards. You may be surprised to learn that many people who are not perfectionist do indeed hold double standards – but in the opposite direction: they hold a more lenient set of standards for themselves and harsher standards for others.

Think about what the impact of holding double standards is for you. For example, is it fair to yourself to have one harsh rule for you that is different from your rule for all other people? How does it make sense that the rules need to be harder for you than for others? What is the impact of double standards on your mood? What people often find is that holding double standards only serves to keep their perfectionism going, as they are expecting more of themselves than other people, and this leads to cycles of strong self-criticism which makes them feel anxious and depressed.

Over-generalizing

Over-generalizing is a thinking style that occurs when someone concludes that because they have failed to achieve one goal this means they are a failure as a person overall. An example of over-generalizing can be seen in Aimee, who went to a lot of effort to clean her house and prepare dinner for her friends: when her cake did not turn out well, she took this to mean that she had failed at the dinner party and then over-generalized this as evidence that she is a failure as a person. Cognitive restructuring can help you to realize when you are over-generalizing, and then help to change this thinking by examining the evidence for your beliefs. For example, what evidence does Aimee have that a lopsided dessert at a dinner party means she is a failure in general as a person? There are many aspects that define someone's worth as a person, and most of us would agree that how well one dessert was presented on one occasion is certainly not a good measure of a person's worth overall. To help you counter over-generalizing in your thinking, it is useful to consider whether the label of being a failure as a person based on one occasion or single performance is justified. How can it be that someone's whole worth as a person could ever be judged on failing to meet one single goal?

'Should' statements

When you have perfectionism it is extremely common to say 'should' to yourself. Aimee's 'should' statements included things like 'I should always have the house perfect' and 'I should never make a mistake when having guests for dinner.' Read through Box 7.7.1 and see if you identify with any of these common 'should' statements, and then complete the blank spaces by thinking of examples of when you say 'I should . . .'.

BOX 7.7.1 EXAMPLES OF 'SHOULD' STATEMENTS IN PERFECTIONISM

I should always push myself to achieve
I should always do things thoroughly
I should never waste time
I should always be productive
I should always be trying to better myself
I should leave as little time as possible for tasks so I don't waste time, even if I am late
I should work harder
I should try to be the best

Examples of my own 'should' statements:

I should

I should

I should

Now you have identified some of your own 'should' statements, how does saying 'should' make you feel? Usually people find that they feel under a lot of pressure from saying 'should', and often feel anxious or stressed as a result. However, saying 'should' does not make our performance better. For example, how often have you said to yourself, or known someone else who has said, 'I should exercise more.' What happens when you think this? Often we feel pressured by 'should' statements, and then criticize ourselves when we do not meet the standard. For example, if this goal becomes a rule – 'I should exercise seven days a week' – it is likely that you will not meet this goal, and then will engage in a lot of self-criticism as a result and even end up avoiding exercise because of the pressure you have put on yourself.

Now consider how things might turn out if you said, 'I would like to exercise regularly if I can.' Does saying 'I would like' make you feel more or less pressured? Replacing 'should' statements with statements based on more flexible ideas such as 'I would like to' or 'I would prefer to' and explicitly acknowledging that 'it is OK if I don't' helps you to feel under less pressure, and so can in fact make us more likely to achieve our goals than when we are constantly saying 'should' to ourselves.

Other unhelpful thinking styles

In addition to the unhelpful thinking styles we have already covered that are particularly strong in perfectionism, there are also a range of other thinking styles that you might notice when you start to become aware of your thinking. These are listed below.

Catastrophizing

This involves thinking of the most terrible possible consequences in a situation and blowing things out of proportion. You can recognize catastrophizing by looking out for statements that start with 'What if . . .'. For example, someone who submitted a report to their boss with a mistake in it might catastrophize: 'What if my boss notices the mistake, and then thinks that I am a terrible employee and fires me? I will not be able to find another job, and I will lose my house and have nowhere to live.' This is ignoring the fact that it is highly unlikely that anyone would lose their job because of one small error in one report; and even if they were to lose their job, it does not mean that they might not find another one, or have nowhere to live.

Emotional reasoning

This is a thinking style where you base your view of a situation on feelings rather than facts. For example, someone who is about to give a presentation might think: 'I feel anxious, therefore I know I will give a bad presentation.' This is basing the predicted outcome of a situation on feelings rather than facts (for example, the fact that they have prepared thoroughly), and does not take into account the fact that many people feel anxious when delivering presentations. Feeling anxious does not necessarily mean they will give a poor presentation.

Labeling

This thinking style involves using very negative and harsh labels about yourself: for example, when you make a mistake, or do not reach a goal, saying to yourself words like 'failure', 'loser', 'stupid', 'useless', 'idiot'. It is very unhelpful to use strong negative labels, and constantly calling yourself such things keeps the cycle of self-criticism going in perfectionism.

Personalization

This involves taking on full responsibility for an event without considering all the other factors involved – in other words, taking on more than a fair share of responsibility for something. For example, an athlete who is playing in a team might think: 'It is my fault that the team did not do well today because I am not performing well,' without considering the evidence that everyone on the team has input in to the final result, which does not depend on any one person.

Mind-reading

In this thinking style we guess what others are thinking without really knowing what they think – for example: 'My boss is thinking that I have done a bad job on the reports because she did not say anything positive about them, and she must think my colleagues' reports were better.' This thought does not acknowledge that the boss may have been busy and not had time to give feedback. The key point is that this person does not *know* directly what her boss thinks of the reports; she is only *guessing*.

Predictive thinking

This is when we make predictions about the future. For example, a student thinking before they sit an exam thinks 'I will fail the exam' despite having no evidence of how they will do. Predictive thinking often ignores contrary evidence from the past, for example, that the student has never failed an exam before and always gets good results.

Did you identify with some of these thinking styles, and think of examples of when you have engaged in these types of thoughts? Now you have read through all of the thinking styles, we will look at how to change them, and any other kinds of unhelpful thoughts, through the tool of cognitive restructuring.

Cognitive restructuring – or, looking at things from a different perspective

'Cognitive' is a word used to denote a thought or belief, and the 'restructuring' involves challenging negative thinking by examining the evidence for a thought. The basic idea behind cognitive restructuring is that thoughts themselves are not facts: we need to examine the evidence for whether particular thoughts that we are having are true and to consider whether there are any other ways to view a situation. At first this can seem a little difficult, as we have often believed what we have been thinking, and taken our thoughts as facts. However, very often our thinking is biased, and when you have perfectionism it can be biased towards being too negative and harsh on yourself – and then you have negative feelings as a result.

Becoming aware of thoughts and feelings

To become aware of your thoughts, it is useful to ask yourself, 'What was going through my mind?' Sometimes thoughts can be statements, such as 'I am a failure', but sometimes you might also have images coming into your mind – for example, when thinking about an upcoming presentation having a mental picture of yourself shaking with anxiety at the lectern. It is useful to write down the thoughts and images that come into your mind.

Feelings are our emotional reactions, the emotional states that we all experience. Some common words to describe feelings can be seen in box below.

COMMON WORDS TO DESCRIBE FEELINGS					
Angry	Sad	Anxious	Frustrated	Happy	Joyful
Nervous	Depressed	Scared	Excited	Irritated	Ashamed

Thought diaries

Thought diaries are used to challenge unhelpful thinking and are an important tool when you are trying to overcome negative thinking. Writing down a thought can help you to gain more distance from the thought and start to see it in a more objective light. The thought diary in Worksheet 7.7.3 includes steps to complete to challenge your thoughts. There is an example included in the worksheet but an explanation of these steps is included below in Box 7.7.3.

BOX 7.7.3 HOW TO COMPLETE A THOUGHT DIARY

1. **Activating event** – Record what was happening at the time you were experiencing strong feelings. It may be an event, or it could be an image or a memory.

2. **Beliefs** – Ask yourself, 'What was going through my mind?' and write down all the thoughts and any thinking styles you can identify. Rate how strongly you believe each thought on a scale of 0–100 (0 = not all, 100 = completely believe it).

3. **Feelings** – This refers to the feelings that are a consequence of your thoughts. Ask yourself, 'What was I feeling?' and rate how strongly you felt it on a scale of 0–100 (0 = not at all, 100 = strongest feeling possible).

4. **Disputation** – Ask yourself questions to challenge the thoughts and get a different perspective on them. Ask yourself: What would a friend say about this thought? How else could I view this situation? Is it helping me to have these thoughts? What positive information am I ignoring?

5. **Evaluate the outcome** – Re-rate how strong your feelings are now.

Now look at the example in Box 7.7.4, which shows an example of how Aimee was able to use cognitive restructuring with a thought diary to challenge her unhelpful thinking about being a failure as a person because of having made a dessert she thought looked bad. Then complete a thought record for yourself in Worksheet 7.7.3. Try to think of a time recently when you felt upset, for example about not meeting a goal, and follow the steps in Box 7.7.3 to challenge your thinking, using the principle of cognitive restructuring to challenge your unhelpful thinking by viewing it from a different perspective.

BOX 7.7.4 AN EXAMPLE OF COGNITIVE RESTRUCTURING: AIMEE'S THOUGHT DIARY

1. **Activating event** (*What was the event, situation, thought, image or memory?*)
Making a cake that looked bad for my dinner party

2. **Beliefs** (*What went through my mind? What does it say about me as a person? Am I using unhelpful thinking styles? Rate 0–100 per cent*)
I have failed as a host and screwed up the dinner party (90 per cent) (*noticing the negative, discounting the positive*)
Because the cake looked wrong I am a bad host and a failure (90 per cent) (*over-generalizing, labeling*)
I should be more careful (70 per cent) (*shoulds*)

3. **Feelings** (*What was I feeling? Rate 0–100 per cent*)
Anxious (95 per cent); sad (50 per cent)

4. **Disputation** (*What would a friend say? Is there another way of viewing this thought?*)
Everyone said they had a good time, and the food was delicious
   One of my friends said the dessert tasted good, and it is taste that is important, not whether it looks perfect.
   I have not failed as a person because of the dessert; the meal overall was very good and the dessert made no difference

5. **Evaluate the outcome** (*How do I feel now?*)
Anxious (60 per cent); sad (30 per cent)

WORKSHEET 7.7.3: THOUGHT DIARY

1. Activating event (*What was the event, situation, thought, image or memory?*)

2. Beliefs (*What went through my mind? What does it say about me as a person? Am I using unhelpful thinking styles? Rate 0–100 per cent*)

3. Feelings (*What was I feeling? Rate 0–100 per cent*)

4. Disputation (*What would a friend say? Is there another way of viewing this thought?*)

5. Evaluate the outcome (*How do I feel now?*)

What did you discover by completing Worksheet 7.7.3? Were you able to identify your unhelpful thinking, and replace it with more helpful, balanced thinking? Did this reduce your negative feelings and strength of belief in the thoughts? You may well find the first time you complete a thought diary quite difficult. That is normal: many people have some trouble the first time they try to challenge their thinking. If you have been having similar thought patterns for a long time, it can feel a little hard at the start to change your way of thinking. But once you have had a little practice, it is much easier to start to view your thoughts in a more objective way. They key is writing the thoughts down, rather than trying to challenge them in your head, and to keep practising.

To really get the hang of challenging your thinking, try completing two or three thought diaries over the next week, doing one whenever you experience some strong emotion. You will probably notice that the same unhelpful thinking styles and similar thoughts come up each time. This is useful, as you can start to come up with helpful alternatives that will apply in more than one situation.

We will consider how to address self-critical thinking in more detail in Chapter 8, which will give you more help in combating unhelpful thinking.

TAKE-HOME MESSAGE

- Unhelpful thinking causes a range of negative feelings and behaviors.
- Common unhelpful thinking styles in perfectionism include all or nothing thinking, noticing the negative while discounting the positive, double standards, over-generalization and shoulds.
- Thoughts are not facts.

- Cognitive restructuring is a tool that can help you to challenge unhelpful thinking by completing thought diaries to consider more balanced ways to think.
- Regular practice and writing down thoughts is important to help change them.

7.8 Procrastination, problem-solving, time management and pleasant events

In this section we will look at how to overcome procrastination; learn a process for problem-solving; consider ways of managing time; and show you the importance of incorporating pleasant events into your life.

Procrastination

Procrastination – delaying and putting off a task until a later time – is a very common behavior that results from perfectionism. Can you think of a time in the past week where you have procrastinated over something you had to do? Is it harder to think of something you didn't put off rather than something you did?! What thoughts were going through your mind about the task that you were putting off? It is likely that you were procrastinating because of worry over doing the task less than perfectly, or concern that you might fail at it? Or perhaps you were thinking that it would take too long to complete the task to your perfect standard, that you might feel overwhelmed while doing the task because you had to do it perfectly, or that if you left the task until the last minute then you would have an excuse if it did not turn out well.

What areas of my life do I procrastinate in?

The first step towards overcoming procrastination is to identify what areas of your life you procrastinate in, and what exactly you do when you procrastinate. This can help you to understand what it is you need to change. To get started, look at the examples of procrastination given in Worksheet 7.8.1; think of which areas of life you have perfectionism in

WORKSHEET 7.8.1: IN WHICH AREAS OF MY LIFE DO I PROCRASTINATE?

Step 1. Circle your area/s of perfectionism
Step 2. Identify examples of your procrastination

Perfectionism area behavior	Example	My procrastination
Eating/shape/weight	Delay trying clothes on	
Social performance	Put off phoning a friend	
Organization	Delay writing 'to do' lists	
House cleanliness, neatness	Delay starting cleaning	
Appearance	Delay ironing clothes	
Artistic performance	Postpone new painting	
Musical performance	Postpone violin practice	
Sporting performance	Put off training	
Academic performance	Ask for extension	
Work performance	Delay starting report	
Intimate relationships	Put off asking for a date	
Parenting	Delaying choice of school	
Health, fitness	Put off going for a walk	
Entertaining	Delay cooking for party	
Other perfectionism areas:		

Reflection on Worksheet 7.8.1:
In what areas do you need to overcome procrastination?

and give an example of how you procrastinate in each area.

Now you have started thinking about the areas in which you procrastinate, you can get a clearer idea about your procrastination by using the technique of self-monitoring that was introduced in Section 7.1. If you remember, in this section we talked about Rob who had perfectionism at work, and procrastinated a lot over writing his sales reports. He would put off writing reports for days on end, but was working longer hours to try to do the reports, although he was actually falling behind at work and sometimes not handing reports to his boss on time due to procrastination.

An example of how Rob was able to self-monitor his procrastination is shown in Box 7.8.1. Using this as a guide, monitor your own procrastination using Worksheet 7.8.2. Because there can be many examples of procrastination behavior even in just one day, you might choose to complete the self-monitoring diary for several examples that happen in one day, or you could complete one example for each day of a week.

BOX 7.8.1 ROB'S SELF-MONITORING OF PROCRASTINATION

Step 1. Record the perfectionism area and situation.

Step 2. Record your perfectionist predictions. Ask yourself: 'What was going through my mind when I decided to delay the task?' Rate how strongly you believe the thought (0 per cent = do not believe; 100 per cent = completely believe).

Step 3. Record your behavior. What did you do?

Step 4. Record your feelings. Examples are: anxious, sad, angry, ashamed, depressed, scared, embarrassed, irritated, happy, disappointed, excited. Rate your feelings (0 per cent = no feeling; 100 per cent = strongest feeling).

Step 1. Perfectionism area and situation
Work: Monday morning, thinking about writing sales reports

Step 2. Perfectionist prediction
I will not be able to write the report to an excellent standard (90 per cent)

Step 3. Procrastination behavior
Each hour looking at the clock and delaying starting report
    Writing detailed 'to do' lists, which has the effect of putting me off starting writing
    Delaying writing because I am distracted by lining up business cards over and over

Step 4. Feelings (rated 0–100 per cent)
Anxious (80 per cent)

Completing this self-monitoring can give you an idea of what areas you are procrastinating in, and the particular things you do when you procrastinate, which can show you what it is you need to change.

Why does procrastination keep happening and how does it maintain perfectionism?

Procrastination is very closely linked to perfectionism – so closely that there is a vicious cycle between the two. To help understand the role procrastination is playing in keeping your perfectionism going, it is useful to understand how you get into vicious cycles of procrastination and perfectionism.

What this means is that the more you procrastinate, the more your perfectionism increases and the more likely you are to procrastinate again, which further increases perfectionism. This vicious cycle can be overcome by understanding how your predictions and self-evaluation based on

WORKSHEET 7.8.2: SELF-MONITORING PROCRASTINATION

Step 1. Record the perfectionism area and situation.

Step 2. Record your perfectionist predictions. Ask yourself: *'What was going through my mind when I decided to delay the task?'* Rate how strongly you believe the thought (0 per cent=do not believe; 100 per cent=completely believe).

Step 3. Record your behavior. What did you do?

Step 4. Record your feelings. Examples are: anxious, sad, angry, ashamed, depressed, scared, embarrassed, irritated, happy, disappointed, excited. Rate your feelings (0 per cent=no feeling; 100 per cent=strongest feeling).

Step 1. Perfectionism area and situation

| |
| |
| |

Step 2. Perfectionist prediction

| |
| |
| |

Step 3. Procrastination behavior

| |
| |
| |

Step 4. Feelings (rated 0–100 per cent)

| |
| |
| |

Reflection on Worksheet 7.8.2:
What did you learn about your procrastination by completing this worksheet?

| |
| |
| |

achievement are intensified by procrastination and then changing your thoughts and behavior.

HOW PROCRASTINATION IS MAINTAINED BY INCREASING BELIEFS IN PERFECTIONIST PREDICTIONS

Procrastination often happens as a result of perfectionist predictions and keeps going because it increases your level of belief in your perfectionist predictions, which makes you more likely to keep procrastinating. Throughout this book we have presented numerous examples of people who have fallen into vicious cycles of procrastination and perfectionism. To help you understand how procrastination keeps going because of increasing belief in perfectionist predictions, we have set some of these examples out in Box 7.8.2. Look at this and then complete Worksheet 7.8.3. Using examples of your own perfectionist predictions and procrastination behaviors, which you have identified in the previous worksheets, try to identify how your procrastination is maintained by increasing belief in your predictions.

HOW PROCRASTINATION KEEPS PERFECTIONISM GOING BY INCREASING SELF-EVALUATION BASED ON ACHIEVEMENT

Now you have started thinking about the strong link between procrastination and perfectionism, it is useful to consider how procrastination also maintains self-evaluation overly based on achievement. This happens because procrastination leads to your feeling you have failed at tasks and therefore are a failure as a person. Take the example of James in Chapter 6, who procrastinated about most tasks to the point that he often rushed them and ended up making silly mistakes. The problem was that because he did make some mistakes, as a result of procrastinating, James felt he was a

BOX 7.8.2 EXAMPLES OF HOW PROCRASTINATION IS MAINTAINED BY INCREASING BELIEF IN PERFECTIONIST PREDICTIONS

Example	Perfectionism area	Perfectionist prediction	Procrastination behaviors	How procrastination keeps going by increasing belief in predictions
Rob (Section 7.1)	Work	I will not be able to write reports to an excellent standard	Delay writing reports; Write detailed lists to delay doing reports; Stare at clock thinking about reports; Line up business cards over and over	The more Rob procrastinated, the less time he had to do reports, thus not doing them to the standard he would like, which increased his belief in his prediction that he would not produce reports to an excellent standard, and made him more likely to procrastinate again
Simon (Chapter 2)	Cleaning	I will not be able to get every room perfectly neat and tidy, so I might as well not start cleaning	Put off cleaning until house becomes very messy	The more Simon put off cleaning, the more he believed his prediction that he would not be able to clean it to his standard, and this made him keep procrastinating
Gemma (Chapter 2)	Study	I will never be able to write a good master's proposal	Sleeping in; Staring at computer trying to think of ideas; Not handing proposal in	The more Gemma procrastinated over doing her proposal, the more she believed her prediction that she would not write a good proposal, and the more she then procrastinated over writing
James (Chapter 6)	Work and social life	If I do not leave things to the last minute, I will get so caught up in checking they are perfect I will not get anything done	Puts off replying to wedding invitation, then makes mistake of forgetting stamp on envelope	The more James procrastinated, the more likely he was to make small mistakes due to rushing, which increased his belief that he needed to check for a long time and made him more likely to procrastinate

WORKSHEET 7.8.3: MY EXAMPLES OF HOW PROCRASTINATION IS MAINTAINED BY INCREASING BELIEF IN PERFECTIONIST PREDICTIONS

Example	Perfectionism area	Perfectionist prediction	Procrastination behaviors	How procrastination keeps going by increasing belief in predictions

Reflection on Worksheet 7.8.3:
What did you learn about how your procrastination is maintained by increasing belief in your predictions?

failure as a person as he was not doing things well. The more he based his self-evaluation on achievement and believing he had to do tasks perfectly, the more likely he was to procrastinate, and the more likely this made it that he would then make some small mistakes, further increasing his sense of failing and needing to do tasks better. Trying to reduce procrastination is helpful in overcoming perfectionism, as it helps to break this vicious cycle and can help to reduce self-evaluation being based on achievement.

What problems does procrastination cause me?

The next step towards overcoming procrastination is to consider the impact it has on you. You can do this by considering the costs and benefits, using Worksheet 7.8.4. Once you have completed a list of costs and benefits, then challenge the benefits, as in the example provided in the worksheet. Often people procrastinate because they feel some benefit from it, for example a reduction in anxiety; but if you examine these perceived benefits more closely you may find that they are not benefits after all, or that they are very short-lived benefits that result in greater costs in the long run. For example, while anxiety may lessen in the short term, procrastination results in increased anxiety over a delayed task that might detract from your performance once the task is started. Also, when you delay a task there may not be enough time left to do it well when you do start, so procrastination can actually reduce the level of performance. It can also lead to feeling overwhelmed as tasks that have been delayed build up. So use this worksheet to examine what procrastination is costing you.

WORKSHEET 7.8.4: CONSIDERING THE COSTS OF PROCRASTINATION AND THE PROBLEMS IT CAUSES ME

Step 1. Consider the benefits and costs of procrastination.
Step 2. Develop challenges for the benefits of procrastination. Ask yourself: Is it really true that these are benefits? What is the impact of these benefits in the longer term?

Benefits of procrastination	Costs of procrastination	Challenge the benefits
Example: Reduces my anxiety	Example: Feel like I am failing because tasks are building up	Example: Procrastination only reduces my anxiety for a short period, and after I have been procrastinating I feel more anxious than before, so it actually increases my anxiety rather than reducing it.

Overcoming procrastination by changing thoughts

Identifying and challenging the thoughts that you have before you procrastinate can help you to overcome procrastination. You can do this using the tools of behavioral experiments (introduced in Section 7.4) and thought records (introduced in Section 7.7). First look at Box 7.8.3, which shows the example of a behavioral experiment that Gemma was able to do to help break her procrastination over writing her Master's proposal. Then design a behavioral experiment to challenge your predictions that are leading you to procrastinate using Worksheet 7.8.5.

BOX 7.8.3 GEMMA'S BEHAVIORAL EXPERIMENT TO OVERCOME PROCRASTINATION

1. **Perfectionist thought:** *I will never be able to write a good Master's proposal*

2. **Prediction in general:** *If I write anything and show my supervisors, they will think I am stupid*

3. **Specify the prediction (specify behaviors and rate intensity of beliefs and emotions):** *I will write something poor (90 per cent), and in the supervision meeting my supervisors will laugh. They will say that I have put no thought into it, and that I do not write clearly. I will feel anxious (80 per cent)*

4. **Experiment:** *Instead of canceling supervision, take in two pages of writing, talk about ideas for the project*

5. **Results:** *The writing was at an acceptable standard (65 per cent). I felt anxious (60 per cent), but my supervisors did not laugh or say I wrote poorly. I have some good ideas now about where to go next*

6. **Reflection:** *I was able to break my procrastination about writing by doing a small amount and I feel confident enough to keep going now*

7. **Revised belief:** *I am finding it very difficult to write my Master's proposal, but it is not true that I will never be able to write it as I have started, and with help I might produce an acceptable proposal (65 per cent)*

WORKSHEET 7.8.5: BEHAVIORAL EXPERIMENT TO OVERCOME PROCRASTINATION

1. Perfectionist thought
2. Prediction in general
3. Specify the prediction (specify behaviors and rate intensity of beliefs and emotions)
4. Experiment
5. Results
6. Reflection
7. Revised belief
Reflection on Worksheet 7.8.5: What did you learn about your procrastination by completing this worksheet?

Now you have done a behavioral experiment to change your procrastination, try also doing a thought record to challenge some of your common unhelpful thoughts that happen when you procrastinate. Again, in Box 7.8.4 you can read the example of how Gemma was able to challenge her unhelpful thinking that was leading her to procrastinate. Complete a thought record of your own to challenge your unhelpful thoughts when you procrastinate using Worksheet 7.8.6.

BOX 7.8.4 GEMMA'S THOUGHT DIARY TO CHALLENGE PROCRASTINATION

1. Activating event (*What was the event, situation, thought, image or memory?*)
Staring at computer thinking about writing my Master's proposal.

2. Consequences (*What was I feeling? Rate 0–100 per cent*)
Anxious (90 per cent); sad (40 per cent).

3. Beliefs (*What went through my mind? What does it say about me as a person? Am I using unhelpful thinking styles? Rate 0–100 per cent*)
I will never be able to write a good master's proposal (90 per cent) (*predictive thinking*).
If I write anything and show my supervisors, they will think I am stupid (80 per cent) (*mind-reading, labeling*).
I am a failure because I am putting off writing the proposal (80 per cent) (*over-generalizing*).

4. Disputation (*What would a friend say? Is there another way of viewing this thought?*)
I was able to make a start of writing two pages, so it is not true that I will never be able to write the proposal. My writing is acceptable. My supervisors have not done anything to indicate that they think I am stupid; they have been encouraging so far. I am not a failure as a person because I am putting off writing the proposal – I will get there, and I have achieved a lot to get so far in my study.

5. Evaluate the outcome (How do I feel now?)
Anxious (45 per cent). Sad (20 per cent).

WORKSHEET 7.8.6: THOUGHT DIARY TO CHALLENGE PROCRASTINATION

1. Activating event (*What was the event, situation, thought, image or memory?*)

2. Consequences (*What was I feeling? Rate 0–100 per cent*)

3. Beliefs (*What went through my mind? What does it say about me as a person? Am I using unhelpful thinking styles? Rate 0–100 per cent*)

4. Disputation (*What would a friend say? Is there another way of viewing this thought?*)

5. Evaluate the outcome (*How do I feel now?*)

As you can see, both of these approaches, behavioral experiments and thought records, can be used to challenge unhelpful thoughts. It is likely that you may need to do a few of each to help break the pattern of procrastination. After you have completed some, put together a 'flashcard' of helpful statements that work for you to overcome procrastination. Box 7.8.5 shows the list Gemma came up with, based on her behavioral experiment and thought record; make your own list using Worksheet 7.8.7.

BOX 7.8.5 GEMMA'S FLASHCARD OF HELPFUL STATEMENTS TO OVERCOME PROCRASTINATION

I'm finding it very difficult to write my master's proposal, but it is not true that I will never be able to write it as I have started, and I will probably do an acceptable proposal

I was able to break my procrastination by doing a small amount of writing and I can do that again, so I can feel more confident about keeping going

I was able to make a start of writing two pages, so it is not true that I will never be able to write the proposal

My writing is acceptable

My supervisors have not done anything to indicate that they think I am stupid; they have been encouraging so far

I am not a failure as a person because I am putting off writing the proposal. I will get there, and I have achieved a lot to get so far in my study

WORKSHEET 7.8.7: FLASHCARD OF HELPFUL STATEMENTS TO OVERCOME PROCRASTINATION

Now you have developed a flashcard of statements that are helpful for you to overcome procrastination, you can also use this list in the 'just do it' approach.

THE 'JUST DO IT' APPROACH

A colleague of ours, Clare, who is well known as being very efficient at work and able to write papers quickly, has an approach which she finds helpful as a reminder not to give in to procrastination. She has a screensaver on her computer which flashes up the words 'just do it'. This is a light-hearted reminder to her, when she might feel like procrastinating, to get on with the task. While this can seem obvious and maybe even a little too simple, it can be quite effective. Look at the list of 'just do it' reminders in Box 7.8.6 and then use Worksheet 7.8.8 to develop your own 'just do it' reminder list, using the costs of procrastination you came up with in Worksheet 7.8.4 and the flashcard of helpful statements in Worksheet 7.8.7.

BOX 7.8.6 SOME EXAMPLES OF 'JUST DO IT' REMINDERS TO HELP OVERCOME PROCRASTINATION

I feel better once I have started something

I feel less anxious once I get going with a task that I am putting off

If I put it off I will feel worse

Getting started writing gives me confidence to keep going

I am not a failure because of procrastinating: if I make a small start I will feel better

Procrastination makes me feel anxious so best not to put things off

WORKSHEET 7.8.8: MY 'JUST DO IT' REMINDERS TO HELP OVERCOME PROCRASTINATION

You can use this list as a quick reminder of why procrastination is not helpful. Some people find it useful to pin up this sheet near their desk, or keep it in a diary or handbag/briefcase to remind themselves when they are likely to procrastinate over a task.

IDENTIFYING AND CHANGING YOUR IMAGE OF COPING WITH A TASK

A final way of changing thoughts that lead to procrastination is to identify the images that come into your mind when you think about doing a task that you want to put off. Often people have a negative image of a task they feel they need to do well. For example, when James thought about doing tasks, he had an image of himself getting stuck at his desk until late at night checking his work over and over and looking anxious. This image was upsetting to James and made him anxious, so he often procrastinated when it popped into his head. James was able to work on overcoming procrastination by recognizing that he often had this image, and changing the image to a more helpful one. He was able to this because, after being able to break procrastination a couple of times by doing behavioral experiments, James could draw on some examples of times when he did not procrastinate to create a new, more helpful image of being able to do the task. When the old unhelpful image popped into his head, James replaced it with an image of himself being able to do an hour of work towards the task, during which he engaged in some checking, but didn't spend the whole time checking, and then stopped work and walked away from his desk and enjoyed catching up with friends after work. He also incorporated into this helpful image the feeling of relief that he had done some work, and the reduced anxiety now that he had less to do at work the following day.

Try to identify the images that pop in to your mind before you procrastinate or when you are procrastinating. Are these helpful images? How could you work to change them so that they are more realistic, and show that in fact you can cope and complete some of the tasks that you feel overwhelmed about and are putting off?

Overcoming procrastination by changing behavior

We have talked a lot about how to change procrastination by changing the thinking that triggers it. Another tool to help reduce procrastination involves practical ways of changing your behavior through breaking down tasks and problem-solving.

BREAKING DOWN TASKS INTO MANAGEABLE CHUNKS TO OVERCOME PROCRASTINATION

This technique involves thinking of a sequence of little tasks, some easier than others, rather than just one big task that is so daunting that you procrastinate rather than getting started on it. Box 7.8.7 shows how Simon used it to overcome his procrastination about cleaning his flat. Have a look at this, then follow the same steps in Worksheet 7.8.9. First, think about what the goal is that you want to achieve. Then think of all the steps that need to be completed towards the goal and break down the task into manageable chunks, rating them for difficulty. Then get started by trying one of the chunks that feels easier.

> ## BOX 7.8.7 HOW SIMON BROKE DOWN THE TASK OF CLEANING HIS FLAT INTO MANAGEABLE CHUNKS TO OVERCOME PROCRASTINATION
>
> **Step 1**: Define the task/goal
> *Clean my flat*
>
> **Step 2**: Break the task down in to manageable chunks and rate chunks from easiest to hardest (0–100)
>
> 0 – Think about problem of procrastinating cleaning my flat
> 10 – Write this list of tasks to be done for cleaning my flat
> 20 – Put away clothes in bedroom
> 30 – Vacuum bedroom
> 40 – Vacuum hallway and lounge
> 50 – Clear items from floor and couch in lounge room
> 60 – Clear books, papers, objects off dining table
> 70 – Put away books and papers in study
> 80 – Mop kitchen floor
> 90 – Clean pantry
> 100 – Clean oven in kitchen

How did you find writing a list of tasks and breaking them down into chunks for a task you have been putting off? You might find that you need more steps for some tasks, or fewer for others, depending on how big the task is. The key is to make each step a manageable chunk that you will be able to achieve. If the step is too hard or has too much in it to do, you may be inclined to keep procrastinating.

Another thing to watch out for when using this practical strategy is that you do not fall into the 'waiting for motivation' trap. I was reminded of this when having a conversation with my 16-year-old niece, whom I was asking about how the girls in her boarding school procrastinate over doing their homework. This was because I could remember

WORKSHEET 7.8.9: BREAKING DOWN TASKS INTO MANAGEABLE CHUNKS TO OVERCOME PROCRASTINATION

Step 1: Define the task/goal
Step 2: Break the task down in to manageable chunks and rate chunks from easiest to hardest (0–100)
0
10
20
30
40
50
60
70
80
90
100

myself at the same age being in the same boarding house and many of us engaging in lengthy procrastination over home-work! She said that if we are going to stop procrastinating then we need to get motivated to achieve the goal, such as doing an assignment. People often procrastinate because they are waiting to feel motivated before they act. Most of us think that motivation comes before action, as seen in Figure 7.8.1. But what we actually know from helping people in therapy who are struggling to get motivated and to stop procrastinating is that it actually works the other way around: it takes action to get motivated, as shown in Figure 7.8.2.

Figure 7.8.1 The common assumed relationship between motivation and action

Figure 7.8.2 The actual relationship between motivation and action

What this basically means is that waiting around for motivation to happen before you act can be a no-win strategy that will end up in you procrastinating; contrary to what many people belief, it takes action to help build up moti-vation. So it is better to get started in the action phase by doing a small, manageable chunk of a task towards the larger goal than to wait for motivation to do the whole thing: that way your motivation will build as each single step is achieved, and then you will be more likely to go on and do more steps towards the overall task.

Problem-solving

Another tool that can help you to overcome procrastination is problem-solving. In fact, problem-solving can be used for any problem you are having, not just procrastination. For example, it can be helpful in working to overcome all or nothing thinking. You might also find it helpful to follow the steps for problem-solving set out below to help you think of other alternatives to overcome your procrastination, or even to help you with the previous tool of breaking down tasks into manageable steps if you are having trouble of thinking of steps.

Look at the steps set out in Box 7.8.8, which shows as an example how Aimee was able to use problem-solving to tackle her habit of spending a long time cleaning before having friends over for dinner. Then follow the same steps in Worksheet 7.8.10 to apply the technique to a problem of your own.

BOX 7.8.8 PROBLEM-SOLVING: THE EXAMPLE OF AIMEE

Step 1. Identify the problem
- try to describe it in an objective and specific way

Friends are coming round for dinner. I need to vacuum the whole house to get it ready, but if I do that I'll be exhausted, stressed and won't enjoy the dinner.

Step 2. Generate potential solutions
- brainstorm all the possible solutions to the problem
- keep listing all the ideas you can think of without judging them as good or bad
- underline two or three solutions that seem the best or most possible to achieve

Ask my partner to do all of the vacuuming; I vacuum only the rooms we will be in; do not vacuum at all; ask partner to vacuum one room and I vacuum the other room.

Step 3. Decide on a solution
- consider the pros and cons of the top two or three solutions – how feasible each one is and how likely it is to solve the problem
- choose the solution that seems best

If I vacuum only the rooms we will be in, it will take less time and I do not have to hassle my partner by asking him to do this. This is the best option.

Step 4. Plan the chosen solution
- plan a list of steps of action that need to be done to achieve the solution

Vacuum only two rooms, put vacuum away and distract from thoughts of needing to do other rooms by starting to do food preparation for the dinner.

Step 5. Carry out the solution

Step 6. Evaluate the result
- What was the effect of carrying out the solution?

I felt less stressed than usual and had more time to enjoy cooking rather than rushing as I would usually do, and my partner said I was more relaxed than usual.

Time management: Balancing achievement and rest time

Many people who focus a great deal on achievement and perfectionism have difficulty in managing time. This can take various forms: being very rushed due to trying to fit too much in; rarely scheduling time for rest or relaxation, due to being focused on always needing to achieve; or procrastinating so that necessary tasks don't get done. If you think you may have difficulty in managing your time, it can be useful to try time management schedules. This can help you to plan out your week in a more effective way, and also help you to

WORKSHEET 7.8.10: PROBLEM-SOLVING

Step 1. Identify the problem
- try to describe it in an objective and specific way

Step 2. Generate potential solutions
- brainstorm all the possible solutions to the problem
- keep listing all the ideas you can think of without judging them as good or bad
- underline two or three solutions that seem the best or most possible to achieve

Step 3. Decide on a solution
- consider the pros and cons of the top two or three solutions – how feasible each one is and how likely it is to solve the problem
- choose the solution that seems best

Step 4. Plan the chosen solution
- plan a list of steps of action that need to be done to achieve the solution

Step 5. Carry out the solution

Step 6. Evaluate the result
What was the effect of carrying out the solution?

Reflection on Worksheet 7.8.10
What did you learn about how you can intervene in your procrastination and perfectionism next time they arise by doing problem-solving?

achieve more balance in life so that not every aspect of your time is devoted to performance and perfectionism.

Think back again to Aimee, who was spending a great deal of time in cleaning and preparing the house whenever she had friends coming for dinner, so that she would often end up rushing and feeling very stressed. Aimee acknowledged that she often put herself under a great deal of pressure, both because of the extra time she spent cleaning her home and because she often stayed late at work. This meant Aimee often felt very stressed as she was not able to fit everything in; and she said her partner would often get frustrated with her as they could never spend time together relaxing as she was always on the go trying to do things, for example cleaning or ordering the house at night, or staying at work until 7 p.m. checking reports.

Aimee was able to use time management strategies to establish a better balance between achievement time and rest time, and also to reduce the extra time she was spending on cleaning, which she recognized was causing problems. She scheduled in time in the evenings to do things like watch TV with her partner and go out to dinner, and time at the weekend for reading magazines and going to the beauty therapist. These were all new things that she would not have done before as she was spending most of her time working and cleaning.

Now try drawing up a time management schedule for yourself for the next week using Worksheet 7.8.11. Remember to try to balance achievement and rest time.

Pleasant events and activities

As a result of perfectionism, people often find that they fall into a habit of not engaging regularly in pleasant events. This may be because they are spending so much time on

WORKSHEET 7.8.11: TIME MANAGEMENT SCHEDULE

	Mon	Tues	Wed	Thur	Fri	Sat	Sun
7–8 a.m.							
8–9							
9–10							
10–11							
11–12							
12–1 p.m.							
1–2							
2–3							
3–4							
4–5							
5–6							
6–7							
7–8							
8–9							
9–10							

Reflection on Worksheet 7.8.11:
What did you learn about how you can manage time to balance achievement and rest? What do you need to do to keep making changes in this area?

achievement and striving to meet goals that they do not have time left to do pleasant events, or because they feel guilty or as if they are wasting time if they do pleasant things that are not directly related to achieving goals. The problem with this is that everyone needs to have pleasant events in their life on a regular basis in order to maintain a balance between achievement and relaxation or fun. It is also important to do pleasant things regularly to keep our mood at a good level. Often we find in therapy that people who have low mood and feel down have stopped doing pleasant events. Doing pleasurable things more often is a simple but effective way to lift mood.

Read through the list of pleasant events and activities in Worksheet 7.8.12 and circle the ones you could try, or start again if you used to do them and have stopped. Also try to come up with some other options that you think you might enjoy, and include these in the blank spaces. These might include things that you previously enjoyed but stopped doing, or something you might always have liked to try, or even something small that might make you feel good and not cost any money.

Now that you have had a chance to think about a range of pleasant things that you could do, add some of them to your time management schedule in Worksheet 7.8.11 for the next week. You might like to think at the end of the week about what impact doing a few pleasant things had on your mood. Did you feel better when doing the pleasant activity event or afterwards? One of the tricks is not to dismiss doing pleasant things as something that is too simple or unlikely to help. When you regularly engage in pleasant activities, you will find that your mood improves.

WORKSHEET 7.8.12: LIST OF PLEASANT EVENTS AND ACTIVITIES

Buy a new CD
Cook a nice meal
Go bike riding
Go to a football game
Learn a language
Watch TV
Listen to a CD
Go swimming
Join a new club
Watch a DVD
Buy a bunch of flowers and arrange them
Play golf
Go for a walk
Have a bath
Plan a holiday
Buy a gift for someone
Play cards
Do meditation
Go on a holiday
Join a book club
Read a magazine
Play tennis
Do a crossword puzzle
Light a candle
Have a coffee at your favourite café
Read a book
Play with a pet
Meet a friend for a meal
Play a board game
Start a new hobby
Listen to the radio
Play squash
Go for a drive
Go to a museum or art gallery
Do woodwork
Go dancing

Play cricket
Go on a picnic
Exercise
Go to the beauty therapist
Play football
Draw or paint
Play a musical instrument
Go to a film
Look at the internet
Go window shopping
Go for a jog
Have friends over for dinner
Go to the park
Sing
Buy something new for the house
Boil cinnamon
Play computer games
Bake a cake
Have a quiet evening at home
Go hiking in the outdoors
Buy some new clothes
Join a community group to help others
Arrange old photos
Phone a friend
Do something nice for someone else
Listen to a relaxation CD
Take time to read the newspaper
Burn scented oils
Email a friend
Do yoga

_____

_____

_____

_____

_____

_____

TAKE-HOME MESSAGE

- Procrastination and perfectionism are strongly linked. Procrastination can increase your perfectionism and intensify self-evaluation based on achievement.
- Procrastination can be overcome by considering the costs and benefits, behavioral experiments, thought records, problem-solving and breaking down tasks into manageable chunks.
- Scheduling time to balance achievement and rest, and engaging in pleasant events, can help to improve mood.

7.9 Putting it all together

We hope that it is clear by now that the strategies in this book are not about 'positive thinking' but are about discovering the reality of your personal situation. Some people with eating problems may have a body image far worse than is the reality. The reality may be that their bodies are neither as flawed as they believe nor approximating the appearance of models. Some people with depression may think that they are useless and a failure. The reality is likely to be that there are some aspects of their lives that have failed, and some that have not. If you have perfectionism, it is critical to find out about your own reality – what it is that you have to accept – and what you have come to believe but is in fact a distortion of reality. The techniques we have described so far aim to help you to discover what is your personal reality that you have to accept.

So far, you may have conducted a survey and found out that most people take only a couple of minutes to make the bed in the morning. You may have conducted a follow-up behavioral experiment and discovered that you felt quite anxious as though things were 'not right' when you took less time to make the bed, and that these feelings decreased over time. You may have conducted another behavioral experiment and found out that procrastination makes things worse for you. You may have taken a step away from your usual way of thinking, and begun to think more flexibly, noticed the positive and found alternative ways of thinking. It may be that you've put all the different methods together (we hope you have) to reach a particular conclusion about your reality. Take the example of Sally.

Sally: Novelist or not?

Sally was a 46-year-old woman who had always wanted to write fiction. She was a journalist on a small national newspaper and had received prizes for her writing at school and university. She wrote the first draft of her novel while still a student aged 21. She had sent it to several publishers, and a few of those encouraged her to refine her story line and develop the novel further. She spent a great deal of time working on the novel at the same time as working in her full-time job, and had a completed first draft when she was 25. She hesitated to send it to publishers again in fear of rejection, but upon persuasion she did so. This time, only two of the publishers even bothered to respond, and they were not particularly enthusiastic. Sally was devastated. She thought that she might need to study writing more, and enrolled in a series of creative writing classes. As the years went by, she continued to work on her novel and attend courses, and occasionally sent the latest draft out to publishers. She felt unable to work on another book until the first had been accepted, and she was also very reluctant to consider that all those years spent on the book might have been 'wasted'. Unsurprisingly Sally was torn. Rationally she knew her novel had little chance of being published, but she also felt unable to give up on her dream. Part of her felt that if only she continued to develop her skills and the story, then someone, somewhere, would publish it and her dreams would come true.

When Sally came for treatment she was depressed and demoralized. She wanted to give up on the novel because she felt that only then could she be free to live her life as she wanted to, but she felt unable to do so. She needed help to accept that it was possible that someone, somewhere, would publish the book but that the cost of pursuing that was too high for her (cost vs benefit). Sadly, she also needed to accept the reality that the time she had spent working on the novel had not achieved the desired goal (to get the book published); however, this didn't necessarily mean it was entirely wasted (all or nothing thinking). She conducted surveys, through which she found out that it was a relatively common experience to invest greatly in something (a music career, a novel, a relationship) that did not materialize, and that the need to 'cut one's losses' was fairly common. By changing her focus on attention to her writing for her job, she was able to see that some of the courses she had attended had been useful, and she had received positive feedback from her colleagues. This enabled her to see that the courses hadn't been entirely wasted.

Sally's reality was that if she continued to pursue her dream of having her novel published, she was likely to continue to feel low and demoralized. There would always be a slight chance that someone, somewhere, would publish it, but there was a greater chance that pursuing her goal would keep her unhappiness going.

Sally's decision was a difficult one. She had invested so much in her novel that it was very difficult to let it go. For her, the choice was between giving up on a dream in exchange for a more mundane reality and pursuing a dream that was causing her significant problems.

Mohammed had a similar dilemma.

Mohammed: Taking risks

Mohammed, aged 32, was a dedicated father and husband with two small children. He worked for the council as a refuse disposal officer. His role was to empty dustbins. He followed health and safety instructions about wearing protective clothing but he was still very concerned about passing on dangerous germs to his children. He was highly perfectionist about his hygiene routines and those of his children and wife. He was particularly concerned that if he passed on anything to his children, then they would miss school and this would affect their job prospects in the future. He met diagnostic criteria for a range of mental health problems including obsessive compulsive disorder, generalized anxiety disorder and depression.

During treatment it was clear that Mohammed was someone who held high moral standards and was determined to do the right thing for his children. He wanted them to have a better life than he and his wife shared, and he was determined to do all he could to help them achieve this.

He regarded this to be his duty as a father, no matter what the personal cost. Conducting surveys was of little relevance to Mohammed, who did not care what other people did but rather was concerned about what he felt was his moral duty, and the best way to take care of his children. It was suggested to him that his children might be more likely to succeed in school (and life) if they had a happy home life and a father they could turn to for advice, and who was not continually stressed and anxious. Mohammed could see the value in this alternative perspective. He conducted behavioral experiments about the best way to help his children – relaxed vs non-relaxed; washing vs allowing them to 'build up immunity'. He began to think in less 'all or nothing' terms and to notice when his children were happy and fulfilled rather than simply focusing on their grades at school. However, although he *could see the merit in this alternative approach, he did not find it made him less anxious; in fact, it made him more anxious. He had begun to realize that giving his children more space meant that they were happier (and that it did not affect their school marks), but he had to accept that this approach carried with it a degree of risk – risk that the children would become ill, risk that they would 'go off the rails'. The alternative, however – an excessive focus on their health and academic achievement – also contained risk. Helping Mohammed realize this and to accept that his approach to parenthood would never be without some uncertainty and risk enabled him to make decisions about his children's welfare with significantly less stress than before.*

We hope that by using the techniques in the book you will have come to discover what the reality is that you need to accept to live a happier, more flexible life. There may be more uncertainty in your life, but that is likely to be compensated for by the new flexibility. We say to our clients that you can always go back to being a perfectionist – but what we hope to have shown you is that you have a choice, some real control over how you live your life.

TAKE-HOME MESSAGE

- The techniques in this book are all designed to be used together to help you discover the reality about your thoughts, feelings and behaviors associated with perfectionism.
- You may have a difficult decision to make, but we hope that by using these techniques, you will be able to make a real choice about how to live your future life.

8

Self-criticism and compassion

In the first chapter of this book we said that unhelpful perfectionism is when your view of yourself is dependent on how well you think you have achieved in areas of life that are important to you, with self-criticism resulting if you think that you have failed to reach your required standards. We know that self-criticism is strongly associated with unhelpful perfectionism. In other words, where one occurs, the other is highly likely to be present. Self-criticism can cause problems in its own right, leading to more perceived daily hassles, more coping by avoidance (that is, rather than trying to deal with or solve the problem, you avoid it and hope it goes away), more negative social interactions and a perception of less social support, and increased levels of depression.

What does self-criticism look like?

Self-criticism can be seen as the internal critic or bully, or the voice in your head that is always pointing out your faults. One of the hallmarks of the critical voice is that it will call you names, like bad, fake, hopeless, loser, useless or failure. Look at the statements set out in Box 8.1: if most of them apply to you, this indicates that the self-critical voice is a strong influence in your head and in your life.

BOX 8.1 AM I SELF-CRITICAL?

- I often find that I don't live up to my own standards or ideals
- I tend to devalue or undersell myself
- I have a difficult time accepting weaknesses in myself
- I tend to be very critical of myself
- If I do well, it is probably because of chance, but if I do badly it is probably my own fault

Why are people self-critical?

The reasons why people can tend to be self-critical vary. It may have originated with the way your parents related to you, if they tended not to reward and reinforce good conduct when you were a child, but were quick to punish you for misbehavior. Alternatively, your discipline as a child may have been unpredictable and inconsistent; in such situations children can learn to blame themselves for anything that goes wrong, as this seems like the most consistent explanation. They then carry this habit with them into adulthood. Whatever the origin of the tendency, many people continue to be self-critical as adults because they believe that it is the only way to motivate themselves to do things and to do them better. In order to consider how useful self-criticism is to you, read the story in Box 8.2 and answer the associated questions.

BOX 8.2 WHICH COACH WOULD YOU CHOOSE?

Imagine that as a parent you took your child along to coaching sessions to teach them to play basketball. It has always been your child's dream to play basketball well, and so they are really excited and determined to try hard in the lessons. Now imagine that your child has lessons under two different coaches: Coach Smith and Coach Jones.

Coach Smith does not say anything every time your child bounces and throws the ball. However, when your child drops the ball or misses a catch, Coach Smith berates them, telling them what a terrible job they are doing, that they are getting it all wrong, and says that they need to try harder because they are just not getting it right. He may also call your child names, such as a 'wimp' and 'pathetic'.

In comparison, Coach Jones does not tell off your child every time they drop the ball but rather encourages the child and says they are doing well when they catch the ball. When your child drops the ball, Coach Jones says things like: 'That doesn't matter, you are only learning; as you keep practising you will get better,' and 'It is OK to make mistakes because it helps us to learn how to do it better.'

Now, when it comes to choosing which coach you want to go on teaching your child, which coach would you choose? Importantly, which coach do you think would get a better performance out of your child – Coach Smith or Coach Jones?

Source: adapted from Pollack and Otto (2000)

It is highly likely that you have chosen Coach Jones for your child. Why is this? We know that when people are continually criticized, it can damage their self-esteem and decrease their motivation, leading them to stop trying in order to avoid the criticism. When we are praised, on the other hand, we tend to try harder and work better. Thus most people would agree that Coach Jones would be more likely to get a better performance out of a child.

It is likely that for most of your life the way you have talked to yourself sounds more like Coach Smith – that you have called yourself names and criticized yourself for making mistakes, ignoring the times when you have done well. Just like the child in the story in the box, learning how you can strive to achieve without criticizing yourself will ultimately lead to a better performance. It is not about lowering your standards, but about deciding which coach you want to have for yourself – Coach Smith, the critical voice who will berate you and ignore your achievements, thus leading to a self-defeating cycle where your motivation and performance are impaired; or Coach Jones, the compassionate voice, who will recognize when you are trying and encourage you to learn from your mistakes, thus improving your performance over time.

What is the goal?

When trying to change your self-critical voice and decrease self-criticism in your life, the ultimate goal is not to stop yourself from ever being self-critical again. This is not realistic, given that you have probably had a lifetime of listening to the self-critical voice. Also, it is important to realize that all people have a critical voice; it's just that most of the time many of them don't choose to listen to it or don't choose to take its messages to heart. Setting yourself the goal of not having a critical voice will just give you one more thing to criticize yourself about the first time you encounter the critical voice! Therefore the goal is to *decrease the power of the self-critical voice*. Imagine the volume control on a radio that can be turned down but not off – the aim is to turn down the volume of the self-critical voice. At the same time, we want to *increase the power of the compassionate voice* – in other words, turn up the volume of the compassionate voice. The next section leads you through a three-step procedure for working towards these goals.

How do I turn down the self-critical voice and turn up the compassionate voice?

Step 1: Identify the critical voice

Go back to Section 7.1 on 'identifying problem areas' and look through your completed Worksheet 7.1.2. In the column called 'Perfectionism thoughts', see if you can identify those thoughts that express criticism of you. One way to help you identify these is to look for the thoughts that you would hesitate to say to another person, because they sound judgmental and critical. When you have been used to being self-critical, it can sometimes be hard to recognize the self-critical voice because you accept it as 'truth' or how things really are. Therefore it can be helpful to note the terms or names you call yourself that appear most frequently, as this will alert you to the self-critical voice more quickly when it speaks up in the future.

Now, for the next week, keep a diary or monitoring sheet that relates specifically to these self-critical thoughts, using Worksheet 8.1. The first column, headed 'Triggering events', is where you put whatever immediately preceded the self-critical thought. It may be a strong feeling that you experience that first alerts you to the fact that you are having a self-critical thought. Reflect on what may have been happening to trigger the feeling. The second column, headed 'Self-critical thoughts', is where you write the self-critical thought that you have in your mind. *In particular*, note when you over-generalize *from* your perceived lack of performance, or the times when you do not stick to the rules that you have imposed on yourself for achieving a certain goal, *to* an unfavorable judgment on yourself as a person. To help you with this, an example from Gemma's case is provided below.

Gemma: An unfavorable judgment of herself as a person

Gemma, a university student aged 28, noticed that she felt most upset when she listened to other students answering questions in tutorials. She felt that she was

> *incapable of sounding intellectual, confident or verbally polished. She avoided answering questions because she thought: 'I am stupid because I can't sound that knowledgeable in my answers.'*

The third column, headed 'Associated feelings', asks you to describe how you felt (e.g. sad, ashamed, angry, depressed) and to rate the strength of that feeling from 0 per cent to 100 per cent. Your feelings can give you a clue as to whether self-criticism is productive or not. If you are feeling ashamed or depressed, it is unlikely that determination to achieve will follow. Rather, it is likely that you will feel less motivated to try again.

Step 2: Identify the compassionate voice

When people have been listening to the critical voice for a long time, they can find it very hard to identify their own compassionate voice. One way to help you tune in to your compassionate voice is to think about the values you apply to your friends and the people you care about in your relationships with them. Look at Worksheet 8.2 and circle those values that are of importance to you with respect to the way you treat your friends, and add any others you can think of in the empty boxes.

Now think about whether you apply any of those values to yourself or whether you do not. Think how different your life would look if you applied the same values to yourself. Worksheet 8.3 on page 229 shows some suggestions about how you might apply the same values you use with friends to yourself. Add in your own ideas and values in the blank boxes.

Now for another month use a new monitoring diary, as shown in Worksheet 8.4, with an example. The first three

WORKSHEET 8.1: DIARY TO HELP IDENTIFY THE SELF-CRITICAL THOUGHTS

Triggering events	Self-critical thoughts	Associated feelings
Can be something someone does, something you do, or an upsetting image	What went through your mind? What does it say about you as a person?	What did you feel? Rate the strength of the mood from 0 per cent (no feeling at all) to 100 per cent (the strongest you have ever experienced that feeling)

WORKSHEET 8.2: WHAT VALUES ARE IMPORTANT TO YOU IN YOUR FRIENDSHIPS? (Circle all those that apply)

Acceptance *To accept my friends no matter what they do*	**Caring** *To be caring towards others*	**Compassion** *To feel concern for others*
Courtesy *To be polite and considerate to others*	**Forgiveness** *To be forgiving of others*	**Generosity** *To give people the benefit of the doubt*
Helpfulness *To be helpful to others*	**Hope** *To keep believing in my friends*	**Fun** *To have fun with friends and share a sense of humor with them*
Justice *To treat my friends fairly*	**Service** *To be of service to others*	**Respect** *To treat my friends with respect and not run them down*

WORKSHEET 8.3. APPLYING THE SAME VALUES TO YOURSELF THAT YOU APPLY TO FRIENDS

Acceptance *To accept myself as being intrinsically worthwhile no matter what I achieve*	**Caring** *To be caring towards myself*	**Compassion** *To feel concern for myself when I am feeling bad and not beat myself up*
Courtesy *To be considerate of myself*	**Forgiveness** *To be forgiving of myself*	**Generosity** *To give myself the benefit of the doubt*
Helpfulness *To be helpful to myself, acknowledging that criticizing myself doesn't get the best out of me*	**Hope** *To keep believing in myself even when I don't perform as well as I would like*	**Fun** *Not to take myself too seriously but be able to laugh at myself*
Justice *To treat myself fairly and focus not just on what I do that is wrong or not good enough but on what I like about myself*	**Service** *To be of service to myself by offering support rather than criticism*	**Respect** *To treat myself with respect and not run myself down*

columns are the same as Worksheet 8.1, but two columns have been added. In the column headed 'What does the compassionate voice say?' use your knowledge of the values you apply to friends to write a specific message from the compassionate voice, which will sound like something you would say to a friend. Alternatively, returning to our coach story at the beginning of this chapter, think what you would want to say if you were talking to a child of yours. Rate your belief in that thought. At this stage your belief may be low, and much lower than your belief in your self-critical thought, but that is fine. Like any muscle group in your body, the compassionate voice will only get stronger the more it is used, and the self-critical voice will get weaker the less it is used. This takes time and practice. Imagine you were preparing to go for a cycling trip in your holidays – if you haven't been doing any cycling for quite a while, you don't expect to just start cycling on your holiday. Rather, you would practice beforehand, and start cycling near where you live in order to build up the muscles required to stay in the saddle for a few hours and keep pushing the pedals. After practicing over time, it feels easier to go further and faster. It is the same with the compassionate voice. As it gets exercised more, it will become stronger and more believable, and the unfairness of the self-critical voice will become more apparent. Thus you will be more likely to question the validity of the self-critical thought, and believe it less.

In the final column you will see that you are asked to rate the strength of the associated feeling once more after having identified the compassionate voice. Once again, initially this may not make a major change in your feelings, but *any* reduction of negative feelings will free you to achieve more and paralyze yourself less with criticism.

Triggering events	Self-critical thoughts	Associated feelings	What does the compassionate voice say?	What has happened to your first feelings when you think this?
Can be something someone does, something you do, or may be a strong feeling or upsetting image	What went through your mind? What does it say about you as a person? Degree of belief in the thought from 0 per cent (not at all) to 100 per cent (completely believe it, no doubt at all)	What did you feel? Rate the strength of the mood from 0 per cent (no feeling at all) to 100 per cent (the strongest you have ever experienced that feeling)	What would you say to a friend? Degree of belief in the thought (0 per cent to 100 per cent)	Rate the strength of the feeling you wrote down in the third column – what strength is it now?
A student's mother complained about my teaching, saying her child was not learning satisfactorily	I am useless (90 per cent) I am a fraud (85 per cent)	Depressed (95 per cent) Humiliated (100 per cent)	This is the only complaint you have received this year – three parents have thanked you for your work with their children (100 per cent) You can't please everyone all the time, no matter how good a teacher you are (30 per cent)	Depressed (75 per cent) Humiliated (80 per cent)

Step 3: How to react to the critical voice when it starts speaking

Imagine your self-critical voice is like a bully. We know that there are a couple of ways to respond to bullying that can be helpful. The first is to have a practiced response ready to use when the bullying occurs, so that you don't react spontaneously and therefore show that the bully is getting to you. The second is to observe but not react to the bullying. We will examine in turn how each of these strategies might help you in combating your critical voice.

When the self-critical voice is dominating, it is difficult to remember or hear the compassionate voice. Therefore it can be very helpful to have the compassionate voice written down, in order to make it much more salient and audible. In order to have a practiced and helpful response to use when your critical voice is loud, you will need to identify the types of compassionate thoughts that most helped your mood and motivation in the diary (Worksheet 8.4) that you were keeping. Write out the most helpful thoughts on small index cards, or even pieces of paper the size of a business card. There should be just one thought per card. You can carry these around with you in your purse or wallet so that they are readily available no matter where you are. You can also put them up around the house, on a wall or fridge, if you do not mind other people seeing them. Over the page are some examples of the compassionate voice that may be helpful ways to respond to the self-critical voice. It may also be helpful to say the words on the cards out loud at times (when no one else is around) as this may help the compassionate voice get a firmer hold in your mind.

The self-critical voice is always going to look for the worst – that doesn't make it true or a fair reflection of my efforts and abilities.

When I don't achieve the standards I set myself, it doesn't make me any less worthwhile as a person.

I don't judge others based on what they achieve and so I will refuse to judge myself based on what I achieve.

Having and pursuing high standards is fine. Judging myself as being faulty as a person based on reaching these standards will only get in the way of my attaining these standards.

Making mistakes is part of the learning process and the pathway to attaining excellence.

The second way of responding to the self-critical voice is to observe but not to react to it. This is a technique called *acceptance*, which is about experiencing without judging. Acceptance has been found to reduce negative mood states. For example, it decreases depressive episodes in people who experience recurrent depression, and it has also been found to decrease body dissatisfaction.

In some ways, using acceptance to respond to the critical voice is like keeping the first thought diary from this chapter (Worksheet 8.1) in your head. When practicing this technique, you are encouraged simply to observe the self-critical thoughts and feelings that follow when you hear the self-critical voice by bringing them to your awareness and holding them there. One way to relate to unpleasant experiences is to register that they are there, to allow them to be as they are in that moment and simply hold them in awareness.

When practicing this technique it is often helpful to close your eyes, if that feels comfortable for you. The first step is being aware, really aware, of what is going on with you right now. Think of thoughts as if they were projected on the screen at the cinema. You sit, watching the screen, waiting for the thought or image to arise. When it does, you pay attention to it so long as it is there 'on the screen' and then let it go as it passes away. The second step is just to acknowledge the thoughts rather than try to push them away or shut them out, perhaps saying, '*Ah, there you are, that's how it is right now.*' Similarly with sensations in the body: if there are sensations of tension, of holding, or whatever, then encourage awareness of them, simply noting them: '*OK, that is how it is right now.*' It can be helpful to label what the thoughts or sensations are, without having to react to them. For example, you might say to yourself, '*A self-critical thought has just come into my mind*' without having to engage with the thought, or '*A feeling of anxiety has just come in*' without having to engage with the feeling.

You can also think of your thoughts like an old tape or re-run of a film, so that you might say to yourself, '*This is my self-criticism tape again.*' This helps us to recognize the repetitive nature of our self-critical thoughts, without necessarily having to engage with them or listen to them. It is a bit like listening to a radio station. When the self-critical thoughts come on the radio, do you have to choose to turn up the volume and listen to them and give them airplay? Or could you choose to leave the volume on the radio where it is and just wait for the next track to come in, without having to give particular attention to listening in to the self-critical thoughts?

What happens when the self-critical voice gets louder at times?

As you practice these techniques over time, we expect that the compassionate voice will get stronger and the self-critical voice weaker. As we pointed out earlier in this chapter, though, this does not mean that the self-critical voice will disappear. Also, you can expect progress to be uneven: on some days it will be easier to listen to the compassionate voice than on others. You can also expect that over time there will be periods in your life when the self-critical voice starts to become louder again and tries harder to capture your attention. Usually this will indicate that some trigger has occurred in your life that has caused you to feel bad about yourself so that you start listening to the self-critical voice again. It can be helpful to identify the trigger, and to use the problem-solving tool to deal with this, as outlined in Section 7.8 of this book. If there is nothing that can be done about the trigger, you will still benefit from practicing the techniques in this chapter, reintroducing them fully into your life. You can expect them to be effective more quickly, as you have already laid down a foundation on which they can be rebuilt. Above all, don't be disappointed in yourself when the self-critical voice gets louder. This is part of the natural ebb and flow of thoughts in our lives, and each time you experience difficulties and work your way through them, you are consolidating your learning and getting a little further ahead.

TAKE-HOME MESSAGE

- Self-criticism can be seen as the internal critic or bully, or the voice in your head that is always pointing out your faults and calling you names.
- People continue to be self-critical because they believe that it is the only way to motivate themselves to do things and to do things better, but evidence suggests the opposite – that it reduces motivation and performance.
- The goal is to reduce the power of the self-critical voice and increase the power of the compassionate voice – the words you would use if you were talking to someone you cared about.
- There are three steps to reducing the power of the self-critical voice – identifying the self-critical voice, identifying the compassionate voice, and then deciding how to react to the self-critical voice when it occurs rather than being taken in by it.

9

Self-evaluation

In Chapter 6 on 'The costs of changing', we looked briefly at your confidence in your ability to change and how this can be low if you have been used to judging your worth according to your ability to meet your demanding and perhaps unrealistic standards. We call this a 'rule for living' that you have, and it goes something like this: *'If I meet my standards then I am an acceptable person. If I do not meet my standards then I am no good as a person.'*

When someone is a perfectionist, over time they demand higher and higher levels of performance from themselves to the point where they are trying to impose goals on themselves that are actually impossible to reach. In addition, over time the domains in which they seek to achieve can become narrower and narrower, and often they end up judging themselves almost entirely by whether they meet standards in one or two areas of their life (e.g. how they do at work, or their child's performance at school). They feel worthy only when they are doing well in these areas of their life. Conversely, when things are not going well in these areas, the person will feel bad about themselves.

Weakening the link between your judgment of yourself as a person and your achievements

If this sounds familiar in your life, reflect on the disadvantages of living this way. One major disadvantage is that we are literally unable to control all the outcomes in our lives. Consider elite athletes who work hard to ensure high-level performance and think about how many times you have heard of injuries that have occurred for reasons outside their control interfering with their ability to attain their goals. If you judge your self-worth by the attainment of goals that are not always going to be in your control, then you ensure that your self-esteem will be a victim to circumstance. This will be especially true if you choose goals that are progressively more and more difficult and unrealistic and eventually unobtainable.

When seeking to weaken the link between your judgment of yourself as a person and your achievements, the aim is to base at least some of your self-worth on areas of life that can weather the storms that will rage around you, that are independent of achievement, and that are based on who you are and your intrinsic worth as a person.

A further disadvantage of judging your self-worth on achievement in a few areas of your life is that it encourages growth of the critical voice, which promotes strict and inflexible rules, as described in the earlier chapters. For example, you will notice an increase in such words as 'must' and 'should'. Think back to some of your favorite teachers at school, the ones who showed a personal interest in you and wanted you to achieve or attain high standards. Did they help you achieve your goals by being autocratic and tyrannical and telling you what you 'must' and 'should' do? It is more probable that you didn't much like the teachers who did that, and that they inspired rebellion or poorer self-esteem rather than gainful effort. Rather, the teachers who inspired you to try harder were likely to be encouraging in the face of effort rather than achievement, flexible in the goals they set with you, and understanding when these goals were not always met.

> *When seeking to weaken the link between your judgment of yourself as a person and your achievements, the aim is to avoid use of strict and inflexible rules and of 'musts' and 'shoulds', and instead encourage realistic and flexible goals.*

Another disadvantage when you judge yourself on achievement in just a few areas of your life is the 'putting all your eggs into one basket' effect mentioned in Chapter 6. If your life is not going according to plan in these few life domains, then your sense of self-worth will suffer. We all judge ourselves to some extent on what we are achieving in our lives, and it is a wise insurance policy to spread these goals for achievement across many different areas – as well as work, study or artistic or sporting achievement, being a good friend, looking after important relationships, hobbies, your emotional and spiritual health, your community involvement, and so on.*

---

* For more on this topic, see *Overcoming Low Self-Esteem* by Melanie Fennell: full details are in the 'References and further reading' section at the end of this book.

> *When seeking to weaken the link between your judgment of yourself as a person and your achievements, the aim is to base your self-evaluation on as many domains as possible in your life.*

A final disadvantage linked with judging your self-worth by your achievements is that it encourages the growth of what is called 'selective attention'. This was addressed in Section 7.6, where, as you will recall, we looked at how a person with perfectionism pays excessive attention to the times when they feel they have failed or not met their goals. The times when they have achieved something or done well will be dismissed, or given only a scant amount of attention. Some people even consider the goal must have been too easy or not worthwhile if they managed to achieve it. Again, if you imagine the teacher who spends most of their time pointing out their pupils' faults, failings and limitations, you can see that this is likely to have a devastating impact on how you feel about yourself. Conversely, the teacher who spends as much time pointing out what you did well as on where you need to improve will be more likely to inspire better feelings about yourself as a person, which will lead to a steadier effort and better overall performance.

> *When seeking to weaken the link between your judgment of yourself as a person and your achievements, the aim is to notice equally what you do well and what can improve with the next opportunity.*

Hot spots

When trying to understand how the rule *'If I meet my standards then I am an acceptable person. If I do not meet my standards then I am no good as a person'* works specifically in your life, you will need to look for the 'hot spots' – the areas in your life that make you feel particularly bad when they are not going well, or that make you feel particularly good when they are going well.

Consider the diary kept by Stephen (Box 9.1), a 35-year-old architect who has his own firm as well as working part-time and for much lower fees for the government on community projects he considers to be worthwhile. Stephen prides himself on always doing the right thing by other people, and delivering high performance at work. He lives with his girlfriend, and keeps fit by jogging four mornings a week. You can see from Stephen's diary that the domains of work and being a good community citizen are the ones that influence the way he feels about himself as a person. He does not mention any impact of spending time with family or friends, or fitness. While he enjoys and appreciates these areas in his life, they do not consume much of his time and he does not consider any achievements in them as being particularly difficult or worthwhile; so they do not impact on how he feels about himself as a person. When he considered what was important to his self-evaluation, he thought that the key areas were work and his ethical standards for being a good member of the community. He summarized this in an 'If . . . then . . .' statement at the end of his week's diary.

BOX 9.1 STEPHEN'S DIARY TO HELP IDENTIFY THE AREAS OF LIFE HE USES TO EVALUATE HIMSELF

Day	What happened that made you feel particularly good or bad about yourself?	What domain of your life does it represent – e.g. social life, work, education, finances, emotional or spiritual health, close or important relationships, being a good community citizen, valued pastimes, fitness, sport?	Write down what you thought and the words to describe how you felt and rate the intensity of the feelings from 0 to 100.
Monday	Client excited by my initial plans	Work	Another job on the way Pleased (85) and happy (90)
Tuesday	Neighbor angry about fence damage caused by my builder's work on extension	Community citizen	I should have kept a closer eye on the builder. I'm not keeping on top of everything. Depressed (75)
Wednesday	Didn't complete plans for government job as scheduled for meeting next week	Work and community citizen	I should have finished that. Annoyed (90)

Thursday	Ten minutes late for meeting with client due to traffic	Work	I am not doing well enough; I have to try harder. Embarrassed (90) and annoyed (85)
Friday	Didn't get as much done as hoped today at work due to getting a cold	Work	I'm lazy. Annoyed (70) and depressed (85)
Saturday	Spent day completing work not finished during week	Work	Finally, I catch up! Satisfied (85) and pleased (90)
Sunday	Speeding ticket on way to parents for lunch	Community citizen	What an adolescent thing to do! I must make sure not to speed ever again. Embarrassed (90)

If I meet my standards at work and am a good community citizen, then I am an acceptable person.

Use the diary below (Worksheet 9.1) over the next week to determine the areas of your life that you currently use to evaluate yourself and that determine how worthy you feel as a person. At the same time, be aware of the other areas of your life that don't register on the scale in terms of influencing the feelings that you have about yourself. After keeping the diary over the week, see if you can come up with your rule, the 'If . . . then . . .' statement that equates your achievements with your self-worth.

How can I develop new ways of evaluating myself?

Recognizing that your self-worth can be independent of your achievements

It is likely that perfectionism has become a stronger force in your life over time as you have grown older; from your current perspective it may well be difficult to remember a time in your life when perfectionism was not a dominating force. In trying to get back in touch with a life 'before perfectionism' it can be helpful to conduct a historical review of your life and test out your new perspective against what has actually occurred in your life. The example in Box 9.2 shows you how to do this, continuing on with the example of Stephen, and then you have an opportunity to do it for yourself in Worksheet 9.2.

WORKSHEET 9.1: DIARY TO HELP IDENTIFY THE AREAS OF YOUR LIFE THAT YOU CURRENTLY USE TO EVALUATE YOURSELF

Day	What happened that made you feel particularly good or bad about yourself?	What domain of your life does it represent – e.g. social life, work, education, finances, emotional or spiritual health, close or important relationships, being a good community citizen, valued pastimes, fitness, sport?	Write down what you thought and the words to describe how you felt and rate the intensity of the feelings from 0 to 100
Monday	Client excited by my initial plans	Work	Another job on the way Pleased (85) and happy (90)
Tuesday			
Wednesday			
Thursday			
Friday			
Saturday			
Sunday			

If _____ then _____

BOX 9.2 STEPHEN'S HISTORICAL TEST OF THE NEW PERSPECTIVE

New perspective: When I don't achieve the standards I set myself, it doesn't make me any less worthwhile as a person

Age	Experiences I had that are consistent with this new perspective
Birth–2	Photos show Mum and Dad having fun and enjoying time with me and my older sister, even though I wasn't achieving anything but just being a baby and a toddler
3–5	Spending time playing with my best friend down the road – enjoying each other's company
6–11	At school when I was nine I had a difficult year because Mum and Dad had separated and my academic performance slipped; but my class teacher spent time with me, encouraging me and making sure I was OK. My best friend throughout school really enjoyed spending time with me, no matter what was happening in my life or with any achievements at school
12–15	Starting secondary school was difficult, I was a bit of a nerd, but I developed two new friends whom I still see today, who just enjoyed hanging out with me
16–18	I had my first girlfriend – she liked my passion for community service and justice, and she also shared my taste in music, and she didn't care whether I did well at school or got into university
19–25	When I failed one of my architecture exams my friends showed how much they cared about me and took me away for the weekend

WORKSHEET 9.2: MY HISTORICAL TEST OF THE NEW PERSPECTIVE: APPLIED TO ME

New perspective: When I don't achieve the standards I set myself, it doesn't make me any less worthwhile as a person	
Age	*Experiences I had that are consistent with this new perspective*
Birth–2	
3–5	
6–11	
12–15	
16–18	
19–25	

It might make the message of the historical review stronger if you can find some relevant photos of the times or occasions that you refer to, and start your own scrapbook that illustrates this new rule. The scrapbook will remind you that the new rule has been operating in your life previously but has just been overlooked more recently.

Another way of reinforcing this new perspective is to write yourself a letter, taking the perspective of a 'compassionate other'. This could be an abstract person, someone who doesn't exist but has a compassionate nature; or it could be a real person whom you consider to be compassionate but whom you don't know personally, like Mother Teresa or the Dalai Lama; or it could be a real person whom you do know and whom you consider to be compassionate. From this person's perspective, write the letter to yourself, commenting on what the historical review showed about what makes you worthwhile as a person apart from your achievements or meeting your standards.

Encouraging flexible and realistic goals

Another pathway to weakening the link between judging your worth as a person and your achievements is to adopt more flexible and realistic goals. Goals that are flexible do not include the words 'should' and 'must'. An example of an inflexible goal for Stephen was: *'I must always be on time for site meetings.'* An example of a more flexible goal for him is: *'I will always try to be on time for site meetings but realize that I can't control every eventuality all the time and may sometimes be late. I will make sure I have the client's mobile phone number with me in case I need to call them to let them know that I will be late.'*

Goals that are realistic are achievable after reasonable but not superhuman effort. Another of Stephen's unrealistic goals looked something like this: *'I must always complete the work that I have set for myself each day.'* This goal is unrealistic because it doesn't take into account any unscheduled interruptions outside Stephen's control, such as phone calls, unplanned visitors or issues arising with other jobs that are currently running. Also, Stephen may be setting himself too high a workload for each day, one that requires more than the hours in the working day to achieve.

One way of thinking through whether the goals you set yourself are achievable is to conduct a survey, as described in Section 7.3. You would survey people who you consider to have some achievements in their life and whom you admire, but who you also think have some balance in their lives and a good quality of life. Some of the questions you might ask them are: What types of goals do you set yourself each day? What happens when you don't achieve them? How do you cope with that? With this information you can reconsider your own goals.

Stephen surveyed two colleagues of his who were architects and with whom he had gone through university. He knew that they had a good reputation and he admired much of the work they had done. After talking with them, he realized that although they set themselves ambitious goals for workload each day, their goals were a little less ambitious, and more obtainable, than his goals. Therefore they were less frustrated at the end of each day. In addition, they treated their goals as guidelines to help them keep the work moving, but not absolutes that had to be achieved that day. They also were more successful in allocating work to other people when they were under pressure, rather than keeping all the work to themselves and trying to spend even more time on trying to complete the work. Stephen found it helpful to get these perspectives and reconsidered some of his work practices in the light of this information.

Spreading your self-evaluation across as many areas of your life as possible

You started thinking about spreading out your self-evaluation more widely over different areas of life in Chapter 8. Now we can return to these ideas and take them forward another step. Look at Worksheet 9.3, which is similar to the chart you completed in Chapter 6 as Worksheet 6.4. Since last doing this exercise you have been considering many issues and practicing ways of standing up to perfectionism and the critical voice. Complete the exercise again and compare how if differs from what you did earlier. What new ideas or issues or goals have emerged?

Now select four life areas that are different from those you identified at the beginning of this chapter that you currently use to evaluate your self-worth. Choose the four that appeal to you most and which you consider have the potential to contribute to, and expand, the way you evaluate yourself. Using Worksheet 9.4, set yourself some specific short-term goals (i.e. goals that can be achieved within a six-month period) in each of these four life areas. Some examples could include spending more time with certain people, or developing a pastime for enjoyment rather than achievement, or returning to hobbies that you have had in the past that have been neglected as you focused on achievement in fewer areas.

As you select the goals, keep in mind the issues discussed above with respect to choosing flexible and realistic goals, and avoid any use of 'must' or 'should'. It may also be helpful to check with other people to see if they consider these goals attainable within six months. At this stage, choose small steps rather than large ones, as the idea is to start expanding some areas in your life, not to master a whole new area of life overnight.

WORKSHEET 9.3: EXPANDING MY SELF-EVALUATION ACROSS DIFFERENT LIFE AREAS

Area of life	Who do you want to be in this area? What do you want to do in this area?
My social life	
My work/education	
My finances	
My emotional health	
My relationship with my partner	
My relationships with my children	
My relationships with close friends	
My relationships with my parents/siblings	
My contribution to the community	
My spiritual life	
My valued pastimes and hobbies	
My fitness and physical and nutritional health	
Other (please specify)	

WORKSHEET 9.4: GOALS TO WORK ON FOR THE NEXT SIX MONTHS THAT WILL EXPAND THE AREAS OF MY LIFE THAT CONTRIBUTE TO MY SELF-WORTH (1)

Life area 1	
The changes I want to make are:	
The most important reasons I want to make these changes are:	
The steps I plan to take are:	
I will know that my plan is working if:	
Things that might interfere with my plan and how I will overcome them are:	
Life area 2	
The changes I want to make are:	
The most important reasons I want to make these changes are:	
The steps I plan to take are:	
I will know that my plan is working if:	
Things that might interfere with my plan and how I will overcome them are:	

WORKSHEET 9.4: GOALS TO WORK ON FOR THE NEXT SIX MONTHS THAT WILL EXPAND THE AREAS OF MY LIFE THAT CONTRIBUTE TO MY SELF-WORTH (2)

Life area 3	
The changes I want to make are:	
The most important reasons I want to make these changes are:	
The steps I plan to take are:	
I will know that my plan is working if:	
Things that might interfere with my plan and how I will overcome them are:	
Life area 4	
The changes I want to make are:	
The most important reasons I want to make these changes are:	
The steps I plan to take are:	
I will know that my plan is working if:	
Things that might interfere with my plan and how I will overcome them are:	

Develop more balance in what you pay attention to on a day-to-day basis

The final step to consider in the process of weakening the link between judging your worth as a person and your achievements is to develop more balance in what you pay attention to as you go through your days. Perfectionists get used to paying attention to what they don't do, or don't achieve, or when they perform less well than they planned. However, they pay little attention to what they are doing well.

A simple way of retraining your attention is to keep a daily log in which you note down each day at least one thing that you have achieved or done on that day. Train yourself to look for the small achievements, in a broad range of areas, including the sorts of things you might normally dismiss. Box 9.3 shows an example from Stephen's daily log.

BOX 9.3 STEPHEN'S DAILY LOG OF ACHIEVEMENTS	
Day	Achievement
Monday	Made time to take the dog for a walk even though I wanted to keep working
Tuesday	Started a job that I had been putting off because I wasn't sure how to proceed
Wednesday	Bought a cake to work to share with others
Thursday	Rang Mum and Dad to see how they were even though I was really busy with work
Friday	Kept my cool in the meeting with a client even though they were being a complete pain
Saturday	Completed the plans for the meeting on Monday
Sunday	Went for a picnic with Jen rather than working as I was tempted to do

Try keeping your own daily log, and remember the general principles:

- pay attention to any achievements, no matter how small or insignificant they might seem to you at the time; and
- note achievements across all areas of your life.

TAKE-HOME MESSAGE

- Longer-term freedom from perfectionism can be helped along by building up a new perspective: *'When I don't achieve the standards I set myself, it doesn't make me any less worthwhile as a person.'*
- Building up this rule in your life can be achieved by
  - recognizing that your self-worth can be independent of your achievements,
  - choosing flexible and realistic goals
  - expanding your self-evaluation across a variety of areas of your life, and
  - paying daily attention to your achievements across all areas of your life, no matter how small they may seem.

10

Freedom

Over the course of this book we have made the case that perfectionist striving is inevitably associated with inflexibility and self-criticism. Ironically, this striving reduces your chances of achieving excellence because it can lead to procrastination, avoidance, fatigue, self-criticism and ultimately damaged self-esteem. Throughout this book we have also made the case that turning the rigid rules that accompany perfectionism into guidelines provides a pathway to flexibility and freedom – greater freedom to pursue excellence, greater freedom to like yourself, greater freedom to be compassionate towards yourself, and greater freedom to enjoy your life.

> *Make a supreme effort to root out self-love from your heart and to plant in its place this holy self-hatred. This is the royal road by which we turn our backs on mediocrity, and which leads us without fail to the summit of perfection.*
>
> St Catherine of Siena (1347–80)

Consider the quote above, from Catherine of Siena. This exhortation illustrates our suggestion that perfectionism and self-criticism (or 'holy self-hatred') go hand in hand. St Catherine's life also offers an example of how being rigidly perfectionist can interfere with your ability to achieve your goals. Her pursuit of perfection resulted in her eating nothing but a spoonful of herbs a day, aside from the Eucharist. Any additional food she was forced to eat she would regurgitate by pushing a twig or small branch down her throat. While she achieved many impressive things, including representations to the Pope of the day about healing schisms in the Church and writing letters considered among the great works of early Tuscan literature, her life was cut short by a stroke at age 33, no doubt as a result of the virtual starvation linked to her perfectionism.

It's the notion that there is no perfection – that there is a broken world and we live with broken hearts and broken lives but still there is no alibi for anything. On the contrary, you have to stand up and say hallelujah under those circumstances.

Leonard Cohen, about the song 'Hallelujah' (1995)

This second quote is from Leonard Cohen, a singer-songwriter, musician, poet, novelist and artist, and illustrates a principle that underlines all that has been written in this book. Perfection is not a realistic or desirable goal; on the contrary, we can celebrate our imperfections and experience greater freedom in our lives as a result. Leonard Cohen's embrace of imperfection has set him free to experiment with goals in his life, sometimes unsuccessfully and sometimes successfully. Twenty-four years after the original release of his song 'Hallelujah', covers of it were placed at numbers one and two in the United Kingdom Christmas singles chart in 2008, with a third release, by Cohen himself, placed at number 36. He is widely acclaimed throughout the world for his musical skill, and was described by Lou Reed as belonging to the 'highest and most influential echelon of songwriters'. His failures have not tarnished his overall reputation and achievements – in fact, these achievements were probably not possible without the failures.

In the end it comes down to a choice. Do you want to keep punishing yourself in pursuit of that impossible goal, reaching the 'summit of perfection'? Or do you want to choose freedom from demanding and inflexible rules and standards in your life? If you have been working towards this latter goal by using the ideas presented in this book, then it is likely that you have started to see changes that have brought you increased freedom and flexibility without any significant deterioration in performance. Indeed, you might have noticed an improved performance. The degree of change experienced will differ from person to person. Keep in mind that even small changes are important. Just as an avalanche can be triggered by one small pebble falling, one small change is able to start a chain reaction in your life because you have started to experience change and believe that it can happen.

If you feel that perfectionism is still interfering significantly with your quality of life, and you are feeling a little stuck, it is important to consider getting professional help. While self-help approaches can be of help to some, they will not be sufficient for all. Working alongside a skilled helper may be the next best step for you.

If you have started to experience benefit from this book, we encourage you to see this as the beginning of a continuing journey, even though you have finished the book. Choosing freedom still involves hard work! You will need to keep working on the ideas in the book in order to experience further change in your life. The process of continuing change is never easy, especially if you have been living with perfectionism for a long time, and sometimes you will feel like giving in and returning to old patterns. In the rest of this final chapter we suggest some ways in which you can maintain and build on your progress throughout the ups and downs.

Develop an action plan

Put aside some time to go back over the book and all the exercises and experiments that you have completed. At the beginning of the book we talked about the strategies in the book being like tools. Some of the tools that you tried you will have found helpful, and some you will have found unhelpful. It is important for you to consider which tools or strategies you have found to be the most helpful, and to have these strategies accessible in your toolbox so that you can keep using them. As you review each chapter, decide whether the tools described there should go in the toolbox, guided by the following two questions:

- What changes have you made that you want to see to continue to develop?
- What areas in your life require further attention?

Then prepare a one-line summary of each strategy that you want to keep practicing.

You should then end up with a list of strategies that you want to keep using in your life, in order to continue your progress. Keep the list in an accessible place, somewhere you will see it often – on the fridge, taped to a mirror, in the biscuit tin, or in your underwear drawer! Keep the book and any useful monitoring sheets accessible in case you need to use them or refer back to them.

Have realistic and compassionate expectations

Be aware that perfectionist, black and white, all or nothing thinking can influence your expectations for your progress, and that the self-critical voice may also comment on your progress. One of the unrealistic expectations that people can apply to themselves with respect to progress is that they must always be improving and never have any lapses or backward steps. Remember, in any situation where there is overall improvement, there are ups and downs, failures and successes, within this overall trend. This is natural, and the down times should not be considered a disaster, or a cause for panic or self-criticism. That is just part of the way we experiment with change and learn what works best for us.

Another unrealistic expectation you may have is that you always have to make progress by yourself and not ask for help. This is another example of all or nothing thinking and the self-critical voice. All of us at some time in our lives need others to help us through difficult patches. It may also be that you need some support from those around you as you make changes – don't expect to be able to do all of the work on your own all of the time.

Dealing with setbacks: Lapses and slippages

At times of stress the temptation to revert back to old coping strategies may be particularly strong. Again, this is a normal experience. However, when setbacks occur it can be hard to think clearly. At these times, refresh your memory of the following points to help you work through what it is you need to do.

- Consider ahead of time (i.e. before something goes wrong) what types of stress and situations might cause problems for you. This will help you to catch the problem more quickly when it occurs.

- Catch the problem as quickly as you can. This is important, as the earlier you start, the easier it will be to work on the problem. Don't just hope that things will get better, or develop a fatalistic philosophy that there is no point in trying to change any more. Importantly, don't panic, as this may interfere with your ability to act. Remember, lapses and slippages will happen. This is all part of the expected pathway to change. Welcome this time as an opportunity to consolidate your learning process.

- As part of harnessing your resources to intervene, it may be necessary to recruit extra support – perhaps from someone in your social network or perhaps from a professional.

- Dig out your action plan and reinstitute it in your life.

- When things are feeling a little more settled, identify the trigger that caused the wobble – if this is something that can be dealt with or problem-solved, then try to tackle it and therefore diminish its ability to cause any further slippages in your life.

- At the end of it all, be compassionate to yourself. Note what you did well despite the adversity and the failures, and congratulate yourself on that.

We wish you the all the best as you continue to journey toward greater freedom and flexibility.

References and further reading

Useful books

Antony, M.M. and Swinson, R.P. (2009). *When Perfect Isn't Good Enough: Strategies for Coping with Perfectionism*, 2nd edn. Oakland, CA, New Harbinger Publications

Cooper, P.J. (2009). *Overcoming Bulimia and Binge-Eating: A Self-Help Guide Using Cognitive Behavioural Techniques*. London, Robinson

Fairburn, C.G. (2008). *Cognitive Behavior Therapy and Eating Disorders*. New York, Guilford

Fairburn, C.G. (1995). *Overcoming Binge Eating*. New York, Guilford Press

Fennell, M. (1999). *Overcoming Low Self-Esteem: A Self-Help Guide Using Cognitive Behavioural Techniques*. London, Robinson

Flett, G.L. and Hewitt, P.L. (2002). *Perfectionism: Theory, Research and Treatment*. Washington DC, APA

Gilbert, P. (2009). *Overcoming Depression: A Self-Help Guide Using Cognitive Behavioural Techniques*. London, Robinson

Hoffman, S.G. and Otto, M.W. (2008). *Cognitive Behavioral Therapy for Social Anxiety Disorder: Evidence-based and Disorder-specific Treatment Techniques* (Practical Clinical Guidebook Series). New York, Routledge.

Otto, M.W. and Pollack, M.H. (2009). *Stopping Anxiety Medication Workbook*, 2nd edn. New York, OUP

Padesky, C.A. and Greenberger, D. (1995). *Mind Over Mood: Change the Way You Feel by Changing the Way You Think.* New York, Guilford Press

Veale, D. and Willson, R. (2005). *Overcoming Obsessive Compulsive Disorder. A self-help guide using cognitive behavioural techniques.* London, Robinson

Essential websites

National Institute for Health and Clinical Excellence: www.nice.org.uk
UK-based organization providing national guidance on public health, health technologies, and clinical practice

National Institute of Mental Health: www.nimh.nih.gov
The National Institute of Mental Health (NIMH) is the largest scientific organization in the world dedicated to research focused on the understanding and treatment of mental health problems

Useful websites

American Association of Behavioral and Cognitive Therapies: www.abct.org
Provides information about cognitive behavioral therapists and training in the UK

The Anxiety–Panic Internet Resource: www.algy.com/anxiety
A self-help resource for those with anxiety disorders

The Australian Association for Cognitive and Behaviour Therapy: www.aacbt.org
Provides information about cognitive behavioral therapists and training in Australia

Beyond Blue: www.beyondblue.org.au
A national Australian initiative which contains a wealth of information about depression

The British Association for Behavioural and Cognitive Psychotherapies: www.babcp.com
Provides information about cognitive behavioral therapists and training in the UK

Centre for Clinical Interventions: www.cci.health.wa.gov.au
This Australian website contains information about a range of psychological problems and includes a range of resources. There is information on building self-esteem and overcoming procrastination

Internet Mental Health: www.mentalhealth.com
Internet Mental Health *is a free encyclopedia of mental health information created by a Canadian psychiatrist, Dr Phillip Long*

The Mental Help Net: www.mentalhelp.net
This website exists to promote mental health and wellness education and advocacy

Mind Over Mood: www.mindovermood.com
A mental health resource for the public featuring the established principles of cognitive behavioral therapy

The MoodGym Training Program: moodgym.anu.edu.au
This training program delivers cognitive behavior therapy for preventing depression

Blank worksheets

WORKSHEET 1.1: QUESTIONS TO HELP DETERMINE IF YOU HAVE
UNHELPFUL PERFECTIONISM

1   Do you continually try your hardest to achieve high standards?

2   Do you focus on what you have *not* achieved rather than what you
    have achieved?

3   Do other people tell you that your standards are too high?

4   Are you very afraid of failing to meet your standards?

5   If you achieve your goal, do you tend to set the standard higher
    next time (e.g. run the race in a faster time)?

6   Do you base your self-esteem on striving and achievement?

7   Do you repeatedly check how well you are doing at meeting your
    goals?

8   Do you keep trying to meet your standards, even if this means that
    you miss out on things or if it is causing other problems?

9   Do you tend to avoid tasks or put off doing them in case you fail or
    because of the time it would take?

WORKSHEET 5.1: QUESTIONS TO HELP YOU DRAW YOUR DIAGRAM OF WHAT IS KEEPING YOUR PERFECTIONISM GOING

Q1. Is how you think about yourself, feel about yourself or judge yourself dependent on achievement or striving? Is it too dependent? Would you feel bad about yourself *as a person* if you did not achieve or strive to achieve high standards? If so, this is likely to be a factor in keeping your perfectionism going, and it can be put at the top of the diagram.

Q2. Do you have excessively high standards? If so, this needs to be in the diagram, and as these demanding standards are likely to stem from how you judge yourself on the basis of striving and achievement, it might go underneath the first point above, connected by a downward arrow.

Q3. Do you have rules to help you achieve your high standards? If so, list some of the most obvious ones and put those into the diagram below 'high standards'.

Q4. Does 'all or nothing thinking' mean that you feel you often don't meet your standards and that you perceive yourself as a failure as a result? If so, put this into the diagram with a recent example.

Q5. Do you react to the perceived failure with self-criticism? If so, this should be in the diagram too, again with examples.

Q6. Put examples of 'counterproductive' behavior such as avoidance, procrastination, repeated checking, being overly detailed or overly thorough, and multi-tasking into your diagram and think about what leads to these. Is it failure to meet your standards? Is it self-criticism? Is it anxiety, low mood or stress? Put in the answers you come up with.

Q7. Think about how anxiety, low mood and stress contribute to the cycle of perfectionism. Add these to the diagram.

Q8. If you do perceive that you sometimes meet your standards, put this in the diagram (as in Figure 4.1), with a recent example. Think about how you react to such success, how long those feelings last and whether you discount your successes. All these features should be in your diagram.

WORKSHEET 6.1: CONSIDERING THE IMPORTANCE OF CHANGING
PERFECTIONISM AND YOUR CONFIDENCE THAT YOU CAN MAKE CHANGES

First think of the importance of changing perfectionism as being a ruler marked from
0 to 10, as shown below, where 0 equals not important at all and 10 equals
extremely important. What score would you give yourself out of 10? Put a circle
round the appropriate number.

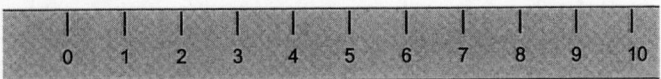

Now ask yourself the following questions:

(1) If the score isn't 0, why not? What are the reasons that change is more
important to you than 0?

(2) If the score is not 10, why not? What would have to happen to make this score
higher? What would you be noticing about yourself if the score was to be
higher? What resources would you have to draw upon to get to the higher
score? What people in your life may be able to help you get there?

Now think of the ruler as indicating your level of confidence in being able to
change, where 0 equals no confidence at all and 10 equals extremely confident.
Decide what score you would you give yourself out of 10 and circle that number.

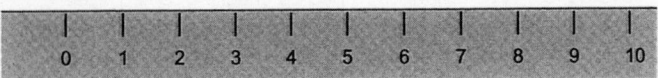

Now ask yourself the following questions:

(3) If the score isn't 0, why not? What are the reasons that your confidence in your
ability to change is greater than 0?

(4) If the score is not 10, why not? What would have to happen to make this score
higher? What would you be noticing about yourself if the score was to be
higher? What resources would you have to draw upon to get to the higher
score? What people in your life may be able to help you get there?

WORKSHEET 6.2: PROS AND CONS OF CHANGING PERFECTIONISM

Advantages of not changing my perfectionism	Disadvantages of not changing my perfectionism
Advantages of changing my perfectionism	Disadvantages of changing my perfectionism

WORKSHEET 6.3: CONSIDERING THE LONG-TERM COSTS AND BENEFITS OF PERFECTIONISM

In one year's time . . . still having perfectionism	
Area of life	*What will have happened in this area?*
My social life	
My work/education	
My finances	
My emotional health	
My relationship with my partner	
My relationships with my children	
My relationships with close friends	
My relationships with my parents/siblings	
My contribution to the community	
My spiritual life	
Other (please specify)	
In one year's time . . . no longer having perfectionism	
Area of life	*What will have happened in this area?*
My social life	
My work/education	
My finances	
My emotional health	
My relationship with my partner	
My relationships with my children	
My relationships with close friends	
My relationships with my parents/siblings	
My contribution to the community	
My spiritual life	
Other (please specify)	

WORKSHEET 6.4: BEING THE PERSON YOU WANT TO BE ACROSS DIFFERENT AREAS OF YOUR LIFE

Area of life	Who do you want to be in this area? What do you want to do in this area?
My social life	
My work/education	
My finances	
My emotional health	
My relationship with my partner	
My relationships with my children	
My relationships with close friends	
My relationships with my parents/siblings	
My contribution to the community	
My spiritual life	
My valued pastimes and hobbies	
My fitness and physical and nutritional health	
Other (please specify)	

WORKSHEET 7.1.1: WHICH AREAS OF PERFECTIONISM APPLY TO ME?

Step 1: Circle each area in which you think you have perfectionism
Step 2: What goes through your mind about this area (thoughts)?
Step 3: What do you do in response to perfectionism in this area (behaviors)?

Area of perfectionism	Thoughts	Behaviors
Eating		
Shape		
Weight		
Social performance		
Checking locks, appliances		
Ordering objects		
Organization		
House cleanliness		
Appearance		
Hygiene		
Artistic performance		
Musical performance		
Sporting performance		
Academic performance		
Work performance		
Intimate relationships		
Parenting		
Health and fitness		
Entertaining		

Reflection on Worksheet 7.1.1
What did you learn about your perfectionism by completing this worksheet?

WORKSHEET 7.1.2: SELF-MONITORING AREAS OF PERFECTIONISM

Over the next week, identify examples of when your perfectionism is a problem.
Step 1: Record both the *area of perfectionism* and *the particular situation*.
Step 2: Record your thoughts. Ask yourself: 'What was going through my mind?'
Rate how strongly you believe the thought: 0 per cent=do not believe at all;
100 per cent=completely believe.
Step 3: Record your behaviors. What did you do?
Step 4: Record your feelings. Examples are: anxious, sad, angry, ashamed,
depressed, scared, embarrassed, irritated, happy, disappointed, excited. Rate your
feelings: 0 per cent=no feeling; 100 per cent=strongest feeling.

Perfectionism area and situation	Perfectionism thoughts	Perfectionism behaviors	Feelings (rate 0–100 per cent)
Work, sending an email to a colleague	I have to be perfectly clear and succinct in how I write the email or I will seem incompetent (90 per cent)	Take 1 hour to check and keep rewording the email to make sure it is just right before sending	Anxious (75 per cent)

Reflection on Worksheet 7.1.2:
What did you learn about your perfectionism by completing this worksheet?

Thought	Emotion	Avoidance	Procrastination	Performance checking	Counterproductive behaviors
I need to write a really good report – it's so important	Fear, anxiety	Not submitting report and asking boss for extension of deadline until following week	Putting off writing the report due at the end of the week, each day worrying but delaying starting	*Testing* – reading comments on previous reports over and over *Comparing* – Reading my colleagues' reports over and over *Reassurance seeking* – Asking my partner repeatedly whether she thinks I can do the report well	Lining up business cards over and over Writing detailed lists daily of tasks to be done towards the report

Reflection on Worksheet 7.1.3:
What did you learn about your perfectionism by completing this worksheet?

WORKSHEET 7.4.1: BEHAVIORAL EXPERIMENT

1. Belief:

2. Identify the prediction in general:

3: Specify the prediction precisely (specify behaviors and rate intensity of beliefs and emotions):

4. Experiment:

5. Results:

6. Reflection:

7. Revised belief:

WORKSHEET 7.5.1: TESTING ALL OR NOTHING BELIEFS WITH A BEHAVIORAL EXPERIMENT

1. Identify your all or nothing belief

2. Identify your prediction in general

3. Specify your prediction precisely (specify behaviors and rate intensity of beliefs and emotions)

4. Create an experiment to test your all or nothing belief

5. Record the results of the experiment

6. Reflection: what have you learned from the experiment?

7. Devise a revised belief

WORKSHEET 7.5.2: TESTING ALL OR NOTHING THINKING WITH CONTINUUMS

1. What is my all or nothing thought?

2. Specify the all or nothing categories on the continuum

3. Examples of when there are points along the continuum in the thought/behavior (is it truly the case that it is completely all or nothing?)

Example 1:

Example 2:

Example 3:

4. What I learned from the continuum:

WORKSHEET 7.5.3: DOING THINGS LESS THAN PERFECTLY WITH A BEHAVIORAL EXPERIMENT

What is my perfectionist belief?

Identify the prediction in general:

Specify the prediction precisely (with ratings from 0–100 per cent):

Experiment:

Results:

Reflection:

Revised belief:

WORKSHEET 7.5.4: REDUCING THE AMOUNT OF TIME SPENT ON A TASK WITH A BEHAVIORAL EXPERIMENT

What is my perfectionist belief?

Identify the prediction in general:

Specify the prediction precisely (with ratings from 0–100 per cent):

Experiment:

Results:

Reflection:

Revised belief:

WORKSHEET 7.6.1: NOTICING THE NEGATIVE AND BROADENING ATTENTION

Step 1. Identify the area of perfectionism.
Step 2. Record the negative thoughts as you notice them, and rate how strongly you believe them on a scale of 0–100 per cent.
Step 3. Identify ways to broaden your attention to include *all* of the information. Ask yourself: (a) What positive aspects of my performance am I missing? (b) How can I focus my attention on things other than negative flaws, e.g. on noticing details around me?
Step 4. Record the outcome of broadening your attention.

1. Identify the area of perfectionism

2. Record negative thoughts and rate strength of belief in them

3. Ways to broaden my attention in the situation

4. Outcome

Reflection on Worksheet 7.6.1:
What did you learn about your perfectionism by completing this worksheet?

WORKSHEET 7.6.2: DIARY OF POSITIVE COMMENTS AND LACK OF
NEGATIVE COMMENTS

Area	Positive evidence	Lack of negative evidence
Work	Boss commented that I did a good job on my presentation	No one criticized the presentation or how I appeared
Appearance	Friend commented that I looked good tonight	No one said that I looked bad
Social	People approached me to talk	No one said I looked anxious or that I was boring

Reflection on Worksheet 7.6.2:
What did you learn about your perfectionism by completing this
worksheet?

WORKSHEET 7.7.3: THOUGHT DIARY

1. Activating event (*What was the event, situation, thought, image or memory?*)

2. Beliefs (*What went through my mind? What does it say about me as a person? Am I using unhelpful thinking styles? Rate 0–100 per cent*)

3. Feelings (*What was I feeling? Rate 0–100 per cent*)

4. Disputation (*What would a friend say? Is there another way of viewing this thought?*)

5. Evaluate the outcome (*How do I feel now?*)

WORKSHEET 7.8.1: IN WHICH AREAS OF MY LIFE DO I PROCRASTINATE?

Step 1. Circle your area/s of perfectionism
Step 2. Identify examples of your procrastination

Perfectionism area behavior	Example	My procrastination
Eating/shape/weight	Delay trying clothes on	
Social performance	Put off phoning a friend	
Organization	Delay writing 'to do' lists	
House cleanliness, neatness	Delay starting cleaning	
Appearance	Delay ironing clothes	
Artistic performance	Postpone new painting	
Musical performance	Postpone violin practice	
Sporting performance	Put off training	
Academic performance	Ask for extension	
Work performance	Delay starting report	
Intimate relationships	Put off asking for a date	
Parenting	Delaying choice of school	
Health, fitness	Put off going for a walk	
Entertaining	Delay cooking for party	
Other perfectionism areas:		

Reflection on Worksheet 7.8.1:
In what areas do you need to overcome procrastination?

WORKSHEET 7.8.2: SELF-MONITORING PROCRASTINATION

Step 1. Record the perfectionism area and situation.

Step 2. Record your perfectionist predictions. Ask yourself: *'What was going through my mind when I decided to delay the task?'* Rate how strongly you believe the thought (0 per cent=do not believe; 100 per cent=completely believe).

Step 3. Record your behavior. What did you do?

Step 4. Record your feelings. Examples are: anxious, sad, angry, ashamed, depressed, scared, embarrassed, irritated, happy, disappointed, excited. Rate your feelings (0 per cent=no feeling; 100 per cent=strongest feeling).

Step 1. Perfectionism area and situation

Step 2. Perfectionist prediction

Step 3. Procrastination behavior

Step 4. Feelings (rated 0–100 per cent)

Reflection on Worksheet 7.8.2:
What did you learn about your procrastination by completing this worksheet?

Example	Perfectionism area	Perfectionist prediction	Procrastination behaviors	How procrastination keeps going by increasing belief in predictions

Reflection on Worksheet 7.8.3:
What did you learn about how your procrastination is maintained by increasing belief in your predictions?

WORKSHEET 7.8.4: CONSIDERING THE COSTS OF
PROCRASTINATION AND THE PROBLEMS IT CAUSES ME

Step 1. Consider the benefits and costs of procrastination.
Step 2. Develop challenges for the benefits of procrastination. Ask yourself: Is it
really true that these are benefits? What is the impact of these benefits in the
longer term?

Benefits of procrastination	Costs of procrastination	Challenge the benefits
Example: Reduces my anxiety	Example: Feel like I am failing because tasks are building up	Example: Procrastination only reduces my anxiety for a short period, and after I have been procrastinating I feel more anxious than before, so it actually increases my anxiety rather than reducing it.

WORKSHEET 7.8.5: BEHAVIORAL EXPERIMENT TO OVERCOME
PROCRASTINATION

1. Perfectionist thought

2. Prediction in general

3. Specify the prediction (specify behaviors and rate intensity of beliefs
and emotions)

4. Experiment

5. Results

6. Reflection

7. Revised belief

Reflection on Worksheet 7.8.5:
What did you learn about your procrastination by completing this
worksheet?

WORKSHEET 7.8.6: THOUGHT DIARY TO CHALLENGE PROCRASTINATION

1. Activating event (*What was the event, situation, thought, image or memory?*)

2. Consequences (*What was I feeling? Rate 0–100 per cent*)

3. Beliefs (*What went through my mind? What does it say about me as a person? Am I using unhelpful thinking styles? Rate 0–100 per cent*)

4. Disputation (*What would a friend say? Is there another way of viewing this thought?*)

5. Evaluate the outcome (*How do I feel now?*)

WORKSHEET 7.8.7: FLASHCARD OF HELPFUL STATEMENTS TO OVERCOME PROCRASTINATION

WORKSHEET 7.8.8: MY 'JUST DO IT' REMINDERS TO HELP OVERCOME PROCRASTINATION

WORKSHEET 7.8.9: BREAKING DOWN TASKS INTO MANAGEABLE
CHUNKS TO OVERCOME PROCRASTINATION

Step 1: Define the task/goal

Step 2: Break the task down in to manageable chunks and rate chunks
from easiest to hardest (0–100)

0	
10	
20	
30	
40	
50	
60	
70	
80	
90	
100	

WORKSHEET 7.8.10: PROBLEM-SOLVING

Step 1. Identify the problem
- try to describe it in an objective and specific way

Step 2. Generate potential solutions
- brainstorm all the possible solutions to the problem
- keep listing all the ideas you can think of without judging them as good or bad
- underline two or three solutions that seem the best or most possible to achieve

Step 3. Decide on a solution
- consider the pros and cons of the top two or three solutions – how feasible each one is and how likely it is to solve the problem
- choose the solution that seems best

Step 4. Plan the chosen solution
- plan a list of steps of action that need to be done to achieve the solution

Step 5. Carry out the solution

Step 6. Evaluate the result
What was the effect of carrying out the solution?

Reflection on Worksheet 7.8.10
What did you learn about how you can intervene in your procrastination and perfectionism next time they arise by doing problem-solving?

WORKSHEET 7.8.11: TIME MANAGEMENT SCHEDULE

	Mon	Tues	Wed	Thur	Fri	Sat	Sun
7–8 a.m.							
8–9							
9–10							
10–11							
11–12							
12–1 p.m.							
1–2							
2–3							
3–4							
4–5							
5–6							
6–7							
7–8							
8–9							
9–10							

Reflection on Worksheet 7.8.11:
What did you learn about how you can manage time to balance achievement and rest? What do you need to do to keep making changes in this area?

WORKSHEET 7.8.12: LIST OF PLEASANT EVENTS AND ACTIVITIES

Buy a new CD
Cook a nice meal
Go bike riding
Go to a football game
Learn a language
Watch TV
Listen to a CD
Go swimming
Join a new club
Watch a DVD
Buy a bunch of flowers and arrange them
Play golf
Go for a walk
Have a bath
Plan a holiday
Buy a gift for someone
Play cards
Do meditation
Go on a holiday
Join a book club
Read a magazine
Play tennis
Do a crossword puzzle
Light a candle
Have a coffee at your favourite café
Read a book
Play with a pet
Meet a friend for a meal
Play a board game
Start a new hobby
Listen to the radio
Play squash
Go for a drive
Go to a museum or art gallery
Do woodwork
Go dancing

Play cricket
Go on a picnic
Exercise
Go to the beauty therapist
Play football
Draw or paint
Play a musical instrument
Go to a film
Look at the internet
Go window shopping
Go for a jog
Have friends over for dinner
Go to the park
Sing
Buy something new for the house
Boil cinnamon
Play computer games
Bake a cake
Have a quiet evening at home
Go hiking in the outdoors
Buy some new clothes
Join a community group to help others
Arrange old photos
Phone a friend
Do something nice for someone else
Listen to a relaxation CD
Take time to read the newspaper
Burn scented oils
Email a friend
Do yoga

_____
_____
_____
_____
_____
_____

WORKSHEET 8.1: DIARY TO HELP IDENTIFY THE SELF-CRITICAL THOUGHTS

Triggering events	Self-critical thoughts	Associated feelings
Can be something someone does, something you do, or an upsetting image	What went through your mind? What does it say about you as a person?	What did you feel? Rate the strength of the mood from 0 per cent (no feeling at all) to 100 per cent (the strongest you have ever experienced that feeling)

WORKSHEET 8.2: WHAT VALUES ARE IMPORTANT TO YOU IN YOUR FRIENDSHIPS? (Circle all those that apply)

Acceptance *To accept my friends no matter what they do*	**Caring** *To be caring towards others*	**Compassion** *To feel concern for others*
Courtesy *To be polite and considerate to others*	**Forgiveness** *To be forgiving of others*	**Generosity** *To give people the benefit of the doubt*
Helpfulness *To be helpful to others*	**Hope** *To keep believing in my friends*	**Fun** *To have fun with friends and share a sense of humor with them*
Justice *To treat my friends fairly*	**Service** *To be of service to others*	**Respect** *To treat my friends with respect and not run them down*

WORKSHEET 8.3. APPLYING THE SAME VALUES TO YOURSELF THAT YOU APPLY TO FRIENDS

Acceptance *To accept myself as being intrinsically worthwhile no matter what I achieve*	**Caring** *To be caring towards myself*	**Compassion** *To feel concern for myself when I am feeling bad and not beat myself up*
Courtesy *To be considerate of myself*	**Forgiveness** *To be forgiving of myself*	**Generosity** *To give myself the benefit of the doubt*
Helpfulness *To be helpful to myself, acknowledging that criticizing myself doesn't get the best out of me*	**Hope** *To keep believing in myself even when I don't perform as well as I would like*	**Fun** *Not to take myself too seriously but be able to laugh at myself*
Justice *To treat myself fairly and focus not just on what I do that is wrong or not good enough but on what I like about myself*	**Service** *To be of service to myself by offering support rather than criticism*	**Respect** *To treat myself with respect and not run myself down*

WORKSHEET 8.4: DIARY TO HELP IDENTIFY THE COMPASSIONATE THOUGHTS

Triggering events	Self-critical thoughts	Associated feelings	What does the compassionate voice say?	What has happened to your first feelings when you think this?
Can be something someone does, something you do, or may be a strong feeling or upsetting image	What went through your mind? What does it say about you as a person? Degree of belief in the thought from 0 per cent (not at all) to 100 per cent (completely believe it, no doubt at all)	What did you feel? Rate the strength of the mood from 0 per cent (no feeling at all) to 100 per cent (the strongest you have ever experienced that feeling)	What would you say to a friend? Degree of belief in the thought (0 per cent to 100 per cent)	Rate the strength of the feeling you wrote down in the third column – what strength is it now?
A student's mother complained about my teaching, saying her child was not learning satisfactorily	I am useless (90 per cent) I am a fraud (85 per cent)	Depressed (95 per cent) Humiliated (100 per cent)	This is the only complaint you have received this year – three parents have thanked you for your work with their children (100 per cent) You can't please everyone all the time, no matter how good a teacher you are (30 per cent)	Depressed (75 per cent) Humiliated (80 per cent)

WORKSHEET 9.1: DIARY TO HELP IDENTIFY THE AREAS OF YOUR LIFE THAT YOU CURRENTLY USE TO EVALUATE YOURSELF

Day	What happened that made you feel particularly good or bad about yourself?	What domain of your life does it represent – e.g. social life, work, education, finances, emotional or spiritual health, close or important relationships, being a good community citizen, valued pastimes, fitness, sport?	Write down what you thought and the words to describe how you felt and rate the intensity of the feelings from 0 to 100
Monday	Client excited by my initial plans	Work	Another job on the way Pleased (85) and happy (90)
Tuesday			
Wednesday			
Thursday			
Friday			
Saturday			
Sunday			

If _____ then _____

WORKSHEET 9.2: MY HISTORICAL TEST OF THE NEW PERSPECTIVE: APPLIED TO ME

New perspective: When I don't achieve the standards I set myself, it doesn't make me any less worthwhile as a person	
Age	*Experiences I had that are consistent with this new perspective*
Birth–2	
3–5	
6–11	
12–15	
16–18	
19–25	

WORKSHEET 9.3: EXPANDING MY SELF-EVALUATION ACROSS DIFFERENT LIFE AREAS

Area of life	Who do you want to be in this area? What do you want to do in this area?
My social life	
My work/education	
My finances	
My emotional health	
My relationship with my partner	
My relationships with my children	
My relationships with close friends	
My relationships with my parents/siblings	
My contribution to the community	
My spiritual life	
My valued pastimes and hobbies	
My fitness and physical and nutritional health	
Other (please specify)	

WORKSHEET 9.4: GOALS TO WORK ON FOR THE NEXT SIX MONTHS
THAT WILL EXPAND THE AREAS OF MY LIFE THAT CONTRIBUTE TO
MY SELF-WORTH (1)

Life area 1	
The changes I want to make are:	
The most important reasons I want to make these changes are:	
The steps I plan to take are:	
I will know that my plan is working if:	
Things that might interfere with my plan and how I will overcome them are:	
Life area 2	
The changes I want to make are:	
The most important reasons I want to make these changes are:	
The steps I plan to take are:	
I will know that my plan is working if:	
Things that might interfere with my plan and how I will overcome them are:	

WORKSHEET 9.4: GOALS TO WORK ON FOR THE NEXT SIX MONTHS THAT WILL EXPAND THE AREAS OF MY LIFE THAT CONTRIBUTE TO MY SELF-WORTH (2)

Life area 3	
The changes I want to make are:	
The most important reasons I want to make these changes are:	
The steps I plan to take are:	
I will know that my plan is working if:	
Things that might interfere with my plan and how I will overcome them are:	
Life area 4	
The changes I want to make are:	
The most important reasons I want to make these changes are:	
The steps I plan to take are:	
I will know that my plan is working if:	
Things that might interfere with my plan and how I will overcome them are:	

Index

Note: page numbers in *italic* refer to illustrations or examples. Where more than one page number is listed against a heading, page numbers in **bold** indicate significant treatment of a subject. The letter 't' after a page number denotes a table.